Archangel
N. Dvina R.
L. Onega
L. Ladoga
Neva R.
Leningrad
Volkov R.
Novgorod
Volga R.
Moscow
Kazan
Kama R.
Duna R.
Ural R.
ARAL SEA
Kiev
Don R.
Volga R.
Astrakhan
Dnieper R.
Dniester R.
MOUNTAINS
SEA OF AZOV
CASPIAN SEA
CAUCASUS MTS.
Bucharest
Danube R.
BLACK SEA
Kura R.
MTS.
Maritsa R.
Constantinople
Halys R.
Tehran
TAURUS MTS.
AEGEAN SEA
Athens
Tigris R.
Euphrates R.
Baghdad
CRETE
CYPRUS
Damascus
N SEA
PERSIAN GULF
Jerusalem
Alexandria
Cairo
Nile R.

THE SHAPE OF EUROPEAN HISTORY

THE SHAPE OF EUROPEAN HISTORY

WILLIAM H. McNEILL

New York
OXFORD UNIVERSITY PRESS
1974

Library of Congress Catalogue Card Number: 73-90359
Printed in the United States of America

PREFACE

This book has an unusual history. In the spring of 1972 Sol Tax, Professor of Anthropology at the University of Chicago, asked me to lunch to talk over his plans for the then up-coming Eleventh International Congress of Anthropological and Ethnological Sciences of which he was program chairman. In course of our conversation he explained his concern at the lack of any overview among European ethnologists and anthropological students of European society. When I confessed that I had in view an essay on *The Shape of European History,* arising from thoughts of my own about the defects of the historiographical tradition to which I had been brought up, he invited me to submit the result to the Congress. I agreed to let him see my manuscript and then decide.

Accordingly, in the summer of 1972 I wrote a first draft of this little book and then showed it to Professor Tax. On consultation, we decided to amputate, offering the three final chapters to the Congress and reserving the full text for separate publication in a form explicitly addressed to historians and students of history. As a result, a session of the Eleventh International Congress of Anthropological and Ethnological Sciences (September 5, 1973) was devoted to discussion of the first draft of Chapters III to V of this essay. They will therefore appear in the Proceedings of the Congress, to be published by Mouton, The Hague, together with a transcript of the comments and discussion of the session.

This publication represents a revised and corrected version, incorporating changes that result from the criticism of the Congress, as well as more extensive alterations arising from the reaction of my colleagues in history at the University of Chicago, Joachim Weintraub and Peter Novick, who kindly read my first draft. That version was also read and discussed with the members of the Workshop in Historical Writing over which I preside; and though my students' comments were usually too polite to count as criticism they were nevertheless often helpful.

As a result of this parturition, the text that follows escapes some of the defects of the original version, since I have profited from others' learning to correct errors. Questionable judgments and formulations still abound nonetheless, and what seems clear and convincing to one pair of eyes will seem absurd or incomplete to another. If this essay provokes its readers into rethinking their views of the shape of European history or makes them reconsider their notions about how to think historically, it will accomplish its purpose, whether or not they agree or disagree with what is written here. An angry, argumentative reader is always much to be preferred to a bored one. For that reason I have retained many passages my critics assailed as incomplete or misleading, believing that brevity and a concise challenge to common notions is more useful than so carefully balanced a statement as to disguise or muffle what I have to say that is new—or seems new to me.

The book is therefore a manifesto, not a masterpiece; the product of a life of teaching and research crossed on a stubbornly sophomoric urge to understand things.

Colebrook, Conn.
September 10, 1973

W. H. McN.

CONTENTS

THE SHAPE OF EUROPEAN HISTORY

I

THE INHERITED SHAPE OF EUROPEAN HISTORY

Europe's history is the history of liberty. This simple and no longer very convincing idea governs the way the English-speaking world conceives the European past despite the fact that few living historians accept the proposition. Yet the way textbooks and standard courses in European history distribute attention among the different regions of Europe in succeeding periods of time can only be explained as a carryover from a time when historians believed, as their successors no longer do, that what mattered in the tangled record of the European past was the piecemeal achievement of civil and political liberty.

This faith continues to pervade American expectations about European history, and does so all the more effectively because we are usually unaware of its abiding presence. German history, for instance, has been a problem for us because the Reichs of Bismarck and of Hitler failed to conform to the pattern of liberal expectation : and the main issue of recent Russian history remains whether or not the revolution of 1917 belongs with the French Revolution of 1789 in the roster of liberating upheavals.

After World War I, generally speaking, historians writing in English ceased to speak of the growth of liberty as the organizing principle for European and/or world history. (In the nineteenth century the two had been conveniently confused by almost everyone.) Thereupon the whole notion swiftly sank from consciousness; yet like an echoing nautilus shell, washed up on the beach after its living inhabitant has disappeared, the stately structure raised at the close of the nineteenth century to accommodate European history still stands. The roof may be leaky and the plumbing deplorable, but in the absence of any alternative housing for unmanageably ample data, the Victorian edifice continues to give shape to what school children as well as graduate students learn and what their teachers choose to emphasize amidst all the buzzing, blooming confusion of the accessible European past.

This essay is intended as an architect's drawing for a modified, more modern house in which, I contend, the proliferating data of European history can find more adequate accommodation.

It is a matter of some importance to link teaching and research, even very detailed research, to an acceptable architectonic vision of the whole. Without such connections, detail becomes mere antiquarianism. Yet while history without detail is inconceivable, without an organizing vision it quickly becomes incomprehensible. To be sure, the organizing vision does not have to be global or continental in scale. For many purposes the national frame, within which most modern history is written, serves well enough. For other purposes, a myriad of alternatives exist. Histories of classes—whether defined by occupation, income, or intellect—and histories of corporate entities other than that of the nation state can usually afford to by-pass any wider setting. To direct attention explicitly to an overarching framework and set of assumptions would merely distract attention from what the historian wishes to convey.

Yet this does not diminish the need for an implicit framework within which national as well as other histories can find a place. Men require such schemes to give meaning to experience. Histories of lesser scale derive significance from their place in the larger scheme, either by illustrating or, more characteristically, by correcting or amending established, general views. In the past half-century or so, professional historians both in the United States and in Great Britain have found it easier to expose the inadequacies of general formulas for describing the past than to generate new and plausible large-scale hypotheses. The result is all too often to reduce professional historical study to trifling elaboration of questions that interest only a small circle of fellow specialists within the profession and leave everybody else completely cold. Erudition of this kind, unconnected with any vivacious hypotheses in which men really believe and upon which they are prepared to act or pass judgement on new experience, is usually dull and is always unimportant.

One can of course argue that things are that way: that human affairs in general and European history in particular are much too complicated to be reducible to any simple, intelligible pattern. But what cannot be understood becomes meaningless, and reasonable men quite properly refuse to pay attention to meaningless matters. What is required for intellectual honesty and vigor is a suitable tension between intelligible overall patterns and the incommensurable or awkwardly commensurable detail.

Unfortunately, absence of an organizing overall hypothesis cannot be remedied at will: someone has to come up with an idea that has enough plausibility to attract serious examination, debate, rebuttal. This cannot be guaranteed. In times past other academic disciplines have faced this difficulty, failed to discover lively, broad hypotheses, and allowed their tradition of learning to decay into an arcane tangle of increasingly meaningless detail. This was, for instance, the fate of classical languages and literature after World War I. Perhaps the study of

European history will follow a similar curve in time to come. Yet there is no law that says this must inevitably be the case. If historians of Europe can discover large-scale interpretations that seem worth defending on the one hand and worth attacking on the other, then, but only then, European history can remain as worthy of attention as in times past.

This essay is intended as an act of faith, seeking to demonstrate the feasibility as well as the importance of explicitly seeking an overall interpretive scheme for European history, one that can bear the weight of contemporary criticism, organize detailed information, and give the subject fresh vigor and value, both for scholars and for the general public.

Before undertaking such an enterprise, however, it seems well to pause briefly and consider how the vision that equated man's past with the progress of liberty came into focus at the end of the nineteenth century. Roots of the idea are very old and lie close to the core of Europe's intellectual heritage. Herodotus (d. 429 B.C.), after all, viewed the Greek victory over Xerxes' invading host as a clear demonstration of the military superiority of free men over "slaves"; and the idea that politically franchised and therefore free citizens were intrinsically superior to men subjected to someone else's will became a fundamental assumption for most subsequent Greek and Latin authors. Even in the latter days of the Roman empire, when political rights were conspicuous for their absence, another sort of freedom grew in importance: for Christian doctrine emphasized the ability of every individual soul to seek salvation through the exercise of divinely implanted free will.

In the fifth century A.D. St Augustine created an enduring, distinctively Christian view of history which remained fundamental for Latin Christendom until the seventeenth century. Augustine emphasized Divine Providence and the mystery whereby each individual's free will in ways that ran far beyond human ken nevertheless remained subject to, and an instrument of, God's purposes for men. During the seventeenth century the development of mathematical physics and astronomy weakened the persuasiveness of Augustine's Providential view of human affairs. As a result, throughout the eighteenth and nineteenth centuries, European philosophers, theologians, and scientists as well as mere historians confronted a serious problem in seeking to find a plausible substitute for the older Christian vision of the meaning and course of human history. Most agreed that history revealed progress, but there was much disagreement as to how progress ought to be defined. By and large, French philosophes of the eighteenth century were mainly impressed by the progress of reason, embodied both abstractly in systematic knowledge and concretely in practical skills. It was left to German philosophers of the early nineteenth century—Georg Wilhelm Friedrich Hegel (d. 1831) above all—to argue that the crown and capstone of human progress was to be found in the advance of freedom. Karl Marx (d. 1883), like other Hegelians, entirely agreed, though he scornfully rejected Hegel's definition of freedom. Then, later in the century, Charles Darwin's (d. 1882) theory of organic evolution offered historians and social theorists what looked like indefeasible scientific authentication of the reality of progress. The only question was how to pick it out from the tangled record of men's past.

Historians set vigorously about the task. On the one hand, they developed their own "scientific" method for comparing and criticizing sources and used these methods to blunt the bias, especially sectarian religious biases, that inhered in most chronicles and histories writen before 1700. In addition, early in the nineteenth century historians applied their new and self-consciously "scientific" methods to a revaluation of Europe's middle ages. Edward Gibbon (d. 1794) (like his humanist predecessors in Italy who had invented the term "middle ages" to describe the decay separating the glories of classical antiquity from their own age), summed up the centuries between the fall of Rome in A.D. 410 and the fall of Constantinople in A.D. 1453 as the "triumph of barbarism and religion." But Johann Gottfried von Herder (d. 1803) and other Germans rebelled against this sort of denigration of their ancestors, seeing the barbarian invasions of the Roman empire as an invigorating infusion of free, if unruly and violent, peoples into an already moribund body politic. In ensuing decades historians set out to trace in painstaking detail how the seeds of representative and Parliamentary institutions had been transmitted from German folk moots to the nation states of the nineteenth century. Such researches proved, at least to the satisfaction of most Germans and Englishmen, how beneficial and necessary the barbarian invasions and the ensuing "Dark Ages" had really been.

From about the middle of the century, a parallel revaluation of what historians soon learned to call "renaissance and reformation" began to take hold. Instead of taking Protestant reformers and their Catholic antagonists on their own terms and fighting afresh the doctrinal battles of the sixteenth century through the pages of history books, as had been customary hitherto, it now became possible to view Italian cultural developments between 1300 and 1600 and European religious struggles of the sixteenth and early seventeenth centuries as part of a much larger movement toward more perfect liberty. Renaissance Italy contributed a sharpened consciousness of individuality in secular matters. This landmark in the liberation of humanity from shackles imposed by medieval collectivities was swiftly followed north of the Alps by the Protestant assertion of individual autonomy and responsibility in relation to God. Taken together, therefore, all the noise and confusion of political and religious controversy, 1300–1650, betrayed a larger meaning: the twin movements of renaissance and reformation, by promoting the development of a population of responsible individual personalities in Europe prepared the way for the enlargement of Europe's political liberties in the eighteenth and nineteenth centuries.

German Protestants and Englishmen found such views especially persuasive. To compensate, the French had their revolution of 1789. That remarkable upheaval provided three generations of liberal Frenchmen, Italians, and a good many other Europeans with a political model and ideal toward which to strive; and when, after 1871 more or less stable forms of parliamentary government came into existence in France, Italy, and adjacent countries, the great Revolution remained a dominating landmark and historical beacon in mankind's advance toward political liberty for those who in whatever form shared the revolutionary aspirations of liberty, equality, fraternity. For a long time, English and German national sentiment resisted recognition of the French Revolution as "a good thing." But by the end of the century, when England and France were about to compromise their long-standing imperial quarrels and join forces in an entente directed against the rising power of Germany, English sentiment became ripe for acceptance of the French Revolution as the central event in continental Europe's modern movement toward a more perfect realization of the age-old ideal of political liberty and individual freedom.

As far as the English-speaking world was concerned, these elements came together in an enormously impressive fashion with the first edition of the *Cambridge Modern History,* published 1901–11. That work, planned by Lord Acton (d. 1902), was thoroughly "scientific" in the sense that its contributors worked from primary sources and showed little obvious religious or even nationalist bias. It made the French Revolution the key event of modern times, the legitimate successor of earlier liberating movements in Europe's past—renaissance, reformation, the Dutch revolt, and the English civil wars.

There was, in addition, another theme: the rise and fall of states and the wars and diplomacy that registered these peripaties. Where liberty, as recognized by Acton and his collaborators, was absent, power took over; but the ups and downs of power had a larger meaning and deeper significance insofar as governments and armies served as instruments, often against their will, or entirely unbeknownst to themselves, of the advance of liberty. Divine Providence in St. Augustine's view of history acted on individual wills in precisely the same mysterious and magistral fashion.

Perfect unanimity among scores of expert contributors was not of course attained; yet the *Cambridge Modern History* did, in its first edition, benefit from a clear general idea of what modern European history was about. As a result, the editors were able to allocate space and define the scope of each contribution with a degree of precision that seems all the more remarkable when contrasted with the confusion arising from the absence of any comparable architectonic vision in the *New Cambridge Modern History,* published 1957–1970. The intrinsic intellectual superiority of the first edition of the *Cambridge Modern History* was magnified by the fact that it appeared at a very propitious time. On both sides of the Atlantic at the start of the twentieth century, teaching of modern history had only recently become professionalized and admitted to school and university curricula. Since teaching the separate histories of every important foreign state was impractical, a common history embracing all the nations that were most active and important on the contemporary scene seemed a necessity.

On the European continent itself this never happened. There modern history meant and continues to mean the study of German, French, Italian, or some other national history. Other nations and peoples figure in the story only as outsiders. They appear as enemies who attacked or foreigners who exploited and oppressed or in some other way intruded upon the development of the nation in question. The marginal position of the English-speaking world in relation to the historical centers of European culture meant that this sort of straightforwardly ethnocentric approach could not satisfy the British and American need for an intelligible history of everything that mattered. The United States lacked a national history of its own that extended far enough back in time to connect securely with the medieval and classical roots of modern civilization; and British history was, after all, insular—and quite self-consciously so. Nineteenth century patriots liked to emphasize the separateness of British history from that of the continent and took smug satisfaction in contrasting Britain's conspicuous success (at least since 1688) in reconciling political liberty with civil order to the erratic and sometimes violent efforts of the French and other continental peoples to do the same thing.

The problem for those who pioneered the formal teaching of modern history in Britain and America therefore was how to reorder the work of continental scholars whose conflicting national biases made simple juxtaposition of one national history with another not only awkward but intellectually impossible. Yet to be scientific it was necessary to take full advantage of the detailed results and professional expertise of French, German, and other research scholars. From the resultant dilemma, the vision of European history as a single meaningful whole, a vision that was implicit in the pages and proportions of the first edition of the *Cambridge Modern History,* offered a triumphant escape. Accordingly, that vision, variously elaborated and modified, swiftly became a basic guide for the construction of courses and textbooks in modern European history for American and British schools and colleges. The basic shape thus assigned to European history still maintains itself in the English-speaking world, more because it has been half forgotten and little examined than because it is any longer actively believed.

This neglect is easy to understand. The bare bones of political and constitutional history, around which the liberal vision of European history draped itself, were further disguised right from the start by attaching other kinds of historical data to the libertarian framework. Cultural history, social history, and economic history all were superimposed upon the original political structure, and in the process the original idea tended to be obscured by a clutter of new, variegated, and sometimes merely miscellanous information. This was the thrust of what James Harvey Robinson proclaimed in 1911 as "the new history"; and in fact the labors of two generations of historians have in large measure been directed toward realizing Robinson's program for further investigation and classroom explication of these facets of human experience. Yet until quite recently all the proliferation of new subject matter and new angles of vision was felt to be desirable and admirable just because, under the surface, there still lurked the organizing principle of liberty, giving form and meaning to the whole. This firm skeleton, even when merely taken for granted so as to be half or even entirely forgotten by new generations of historians, nevertheless endured and imparted to innumerable courses in European history a degree of structural coherence that reassured teachers and students alike.

A powerful Marxian strand entered the English-speaking historical tradition in the 1920's and 1930's. But though Marxists and those influenced by them reversed the valuation placed upon the liberal epos, they did not alter in any essential the patterning of the past propounded by their liberal predecessors. Instead of viewing the contemporary scene with pervasive satisfaction as the fine flowering of centuries of human effort to work out the principles and practice of civil and political liberty, Marxists and their fellow travelers criticized the injustices of the social order they saw around them and often held up liberal political practices to scorn as no more than a facade for capitalist manipulation of public affairs.

Debate and differences of opinion as to the importance of class antagonisms and economic interests in the politics of past ages sometimes became quite heated. Yet in their view of the grand sweep of human history, Marxists remained thoroughly conservative. Like their liberal opponents, Marxists saw all history as unilinear, climaxing in a more perfect liberty. The difference was a matter of timing. For Marxists, true liberty was still a thing of the future. Bourgeois society remained a prison house, and the civil and constitutional restraints on government, of which liberals were so proud, seemed worthless if not deliberately contrived to deceive the proletariat. Hence the tone and emotional timbre of historical writing influenced by Marxism differed strikingly from the rather smug self-satisfaction that had prevailed among English and American historians shaped in the libertarian tradition. But the basic shape of European and world history (Marxists even more boldly than their liberal predecessors projected European patterns on all the world) remained unchanged.

To have structured the historical understanding of some three generations of scholars, students, and men of affairs in the English-speaking world was a great achievement. The men of the nineteenth century who worked out this grand interpretation of the meaning of modern times deserve our warm admiration. Indeed, the vision of the human condition as a long, continuous evolution toward the more perfect self-fulfillment permitted by liberal political institutions ought to rank as one of the major intellectual achievements of the century, offering all who understood the message a persuasive substitute for the older Christian, Providential interpretation of human history, and at the same time reinforcing the legitimacy and sanctioning existing limitations upon governmental activity as these had been developed in Britain and America. In emphasizing the gap that has opened between their views and those that seem adequate today, it is hard not to seem condescending or even scornful, emphasizing the defects and limitations of such a vision of the past. Instead of elaborating criticism, it is juster, perhaps, to try to emulate their achievement by seeking an architectonic vision of our own. Such, at least, is my purpose here.

Perhaps it is unnecessary to insist further upon the value of such an effort at clarification on a grand scale. Yet I cannot forbear pointing out two dimensions of the current scene that seem clearly related to the almost unconsidered persistence of an intellectually unsatisfactory vision of the European past. First, public policy. Ever since 1918 the United States has officially supported the notion that popular self-government is a good thing, and as such should be encouraged to spread from the privileged regions of the earth where it already exists to "backward" peoples where it has hitherto failed to establish itself. This is no more than a vulgarization of the vision of European history worked out by our nineteenth century predecessors. After World War I, President Woodrow Wilson proclaimed his faith in democratic self-government as a sovereign cure for the ills of aristocratic, militaristic central and eastern Europe; after World War II, Presidents Franklin D. Roosevelt and Harry Truman broadened the prescription to include economic development alongside political liberty and extended the formula from Europe to the world. Thereafter, millions of dollars and thousands of experts were mobilized to implement this vision of the future; the wealth and strength of the United States was tapped (even if only marginally) in the hope of promoting freedom and prosperity for all.

Yet it seems clear enough that liberty as understood by Americans or Englishmen has not spread very fast to new lands since 1918. And economic development, when genuinely successful, severely strains the political process by disrupting traditional social and economic relationships. This in turn erodes all the traditional patterns of deference and consensus upon which peaceable adjustment of conflicting interests within a society mainly depends. Indeed, forces are clearly at work that tend to undermine effective representative government, even within the citadels of political liberty recognized by our nineteenth century predecessors. Modern equivalents of the devils Wilson sought to exorcise from the politics of corrupt and jaded Europe have somehow infiltrated the United States itself: secrecy, militarism, authoritarian manipulation of opinion, and the like.

Even in those lands where political parties compete for power and a change of regime after an election can and does happen more or less as a matter of course, it is still true that the public rhetoric of elected officials and legislators stands in flagrant contradiction to their behavior in office; and our intellectual vision of history and the social process at large is so fragmented that it cannot take on the task of modifying prevailing public rhetoric in such a way that official behavior might more nearly conform to what politicians say and what the public really expects. Perhaps, indeed, the sacred aura surrounding invocations of democracy and freedom and the naïve pieties of the national interest, like the no less sacred Marxism of the Soviet Union and other Communist countries, will continue to dominate public rhetoric for generations to come. But insofar as thinking men cannot any longer lend such phrases their full assent, it behooves them to try to offer substitutes, even if men of power and the mass public find such alternatives distasteful or incomprehensible or both.

Nonetheless, it is by offering alternatives and by facilitating shifts of public sensibility that intellectuals earn their keep in society at large. And inasmuch as the assumptions, especially the unspoken assumptions about the past, play such a central part in defining collective consciousness with respect to public affairs, it seems worthwhile making an attempt to clarify overall views about Europe's past. After all, it is from that cradle that our own national culture arose; and the imprint of Europe upon all the other peoples and continents of the globe in recent centuries has been and remains the central fact of modern history everywhere.

A second manifestation of the problems arising from an unsatisfactory overall vision of European and especially of modern European history comes much closer home to professional teachers of history in the English-speaking world. For it appears to be a statistical fact that interest in and positive response to what we have to say has been diminishing among students, and at a rather rapid rate. As far as the United States is concerned, the principal manifestation of this change is the decay of general introductory courses in "Western Civilization" on college campuses. These courses were created at a few pioneer institutions in the 1920's, spread widely during the 1930's, flourished mightily for some two decades thereafter, and then began to unravel and collapse in the 1960's. First the teaching staff lost faith in the value of what such courses had to tell about the past; then academic administrators canceled or modified curricular requirements that had channeled young students into such courses whether or not they chose of their own accord to study the subject; and when requirements were altered, students deserted in droves.

The economic self-interest of historians is very much tied up with this revolt of the classes, for with fewer students there will be fewer jobs for teachers of history—a fact of life already painfully apparent in our graduate schools.

Moreover, if study of history ceases to play the central role in transmitting some sort of familiarity with the high cultural tradition of Western civilization to student generations, the academic discipline of history will, in fact, have lost one of its central roles in our educational system. (The other, I suppose, is to transmit a consciousness of national identity; and here, too, American historians are in some difficulty; but that is another story.) Specialization on the one hand and expansion of scope to new themes and to new parts of the world on the other is no answer. Yet this is what historical scholarship, especially in the United States, has done across the past half-century or more—and with distinguished success.

But multiplication of specialisms and expansion of expertise across a majestic spectrum of times, peoples, and places actually adds to the general confusion. It seems reasonable to suggest, therefore, that unless historians find it possible to think seriously about the overall shape and proportion of their subject, they will have less and less to say to the general public that is worth attending to; and the profession will slowly assimilate itself to the posture and role currently enjoyed by professors and teachers of classics. In such an event, some other discipline or doctrine would, presumably, have to take over the role history played for our nineteenth century predecessors as the means for defining public identities and guiding public policy. Psychology seems the only really vigorous contender for this role. But its theoretical disarray is at least as great as the intellectual confusion prevailing among historians. Moreover, the central insight of nineteenth century thought—that human societies, cultures, truths, sciences, and life in all its dimensions change through time in irreversible and often surprising fashions—is too overpowering, too massive, too obvious for any systematic science that treats time as irrelevant in its reach after an understanding of the human condition to prevail: or so it seems to me.

Hence, the professional self-interest of historians, the intellectual imperatives of the discipline, and the hope of rationalizing the management of our public affairs point in the same direction. All stand to benefit from a clarification of the overall patterning of the course of human history; and a good place to begin is with the history of Europe, since most of the innovations that dominate the world today emerged from that segment of the globe.

This essay, as an effort to provoke reflection upon and to invite clarification of the shape of European history, needs no further apology.

II

HISTORICAL METHOD AND SOCIAL PROCESS

Historians have paid little attention to the general shape of European and other branches of history largely because at the time when the discipline was professionalized a naïve notion of scientific method gained widespread currency in the graduate seminars where young historians were trained. Facts were what mattered; and facts were to found by careful criticism of sources. Once bias and error had been discarded, purified, true facts were left to arrange themselves. At any rate, it was no business of the historian to impose a form upon them, for that would risk introducing a new bias—his own—amongst the facts he had just rescued from that unfortunate condition. Only when all relevant facts had been discovered—or nearly all—did inductive generalization become legitimate. For with *all* the facts before him, a careful historian could let them correct his own personal biases and thus attain truth, pure and undefiled.

Such an ideal imposed sharp limits upon the scope of "scientific" historical research. To assemble all relevant facts is only possible if one sets narrow limits on what one seeks to understand. Hence the monographic ideal: an exhaustive treatment of a tiny subject which can aspire to arrive at lasting, unimpeachable, and scientific Truth because all accessible and relevant facts have been brought under the author's critical consideration. But the question of how a massive array of such monographs could assemble itself into intelligible history was not much considered. Truth was truth, and its grand architectonic was left either to God or to the nature of things.

Practicing historians never conformed to this pseudo-scientific, self-denying ideal. But it influenced all who passed through graduate schools, and did so, in particular, by casting doubt on the reliability and intellectual respectability of large-scale, broadly gauged history. This was reinforced by another, psychological factor. By learning more and more about less and less, an expert can soon outstrip all rivals and remain thereafter secure behind the battlements of his erudition. After all, any rational use of resources inhibits another scholar from retracing someone else's steps in every detail, and, in the absence of conflicting evidence, compels acceptance of the expert's conclusions. Believing that such a procedure was the only scientific way to study history made such narrow specialists doubly secure, since it allowed them to come up with an effective answer to rude outsiders who might reproach them with wasting time on trifles.

As propaedeutic to this essay, which obviously flies in the face of the monographic ideal, it therefore seems well to sketch a different notion of historical method and of social process which is the subject matter of historical study. Those who prefer practice to theory can skip what follows and turn directly to Chapter III.

Men live in society, and society exists by virtue of shared norms of conduct which make individual behavior more or less predictable. No two acts, no two encounters are exactly the same; but the distinctive human invention of language allows men to group varying actual experiences into classes and act accordingly, that is, as if the differences did not matter. This power of generalization allows prompt reaction, and when the criteria through which two differing experiences are lumped together as instances of a common phenomenon are sound, such prompt reactions are also effective, leading to results that are expected and, in a rough way, desired.

Animals undoubtedly share these traits with men, classifying the world into mate, food, and foe as a minimum. What makes the human universe so distinctive is the elaborate classifications we are capable of, thanks to the abstractions language allows; and to the further fact that language itself develops across time as men invent new classificatory refinements, find them useful or amusing, and incorporate them into speech. On top of this, since civilized societies began (and perhaps before that) men have specialized, so that in addition to matters shared with a wider community, various individuals and coteries know things others do not. Such knowledge is both muscular—how to do certain things—and verbal—how to classify and calculate other things. A vast array of technical vocabularies may thus be generated, refining the precision of human reaction to the world indefinitely and with no limit yet in sight.

In trying to understand his specialty, the historian must, like priests of old, try to classify and calculate a segment of observable phenomena—that which reveals something judged to be important about the human past. To do so effectively, the historian must have a set of classifying terms to direct attention amidst the otherwise amorphous and unmanageably bulky materials that record human experience. Any group or individual must start from the classificatory terms he inherits: a private language is useless as well as unattainable. On the other hand, a closely interacting group of specialists, even if few in number, may assign new meanings to old words or invent a set of new terms to accommodate new ideas and point up new distinctions. Such development from an older vocabulary can sometimes proceed very rapidly when experts pursue the implications and applications of a radically new way of organizing their subject.

The study of history, however, has not developed any very distinctive or complex professional vocabulary. This is probably due to the fact that the themes and facts that interest historians most are the same or nearly the same as those that interest men generally. Public affairs, after all, are public; and they remain central to the study of history. This in turn means that historians are likely to find the current vocabulary of their own age for public affairs to be adequate for their purposes and, indeed, inescapable. New distinctions or sensibilities appropriate to the past can nearly always also apply to the current scene, so the possibility of building up a recondite professional historical vocabulary is sharply limited—at least as long as public affairs remain the center of the historian's attention.

There can be no escape from this condition, I think. Language is what it is. Over time it alters little by little; but individuals can depart only slightly from standard usages without inviting crippling misunderstandings.

Yet if one takes the long view and thinks in centuries and millennia rather than in shorter periods of time, it seems clear that in a rather haphazard but statistically effective fashion, languages evolve fresh distinctions and classificatory terms that permit men to react more and more successfully to their environment. Ancient hunters and gatherers did this when someone first noticed a new sort of food and gave it a name so others could be taught to find it. This sort of breakthrough must sometimes have had decisive survival value. A community competing with similar groups in the same or similar landscapes would have a clear edge over neighbors who failed to notice some potential food because they had no name for it.[1]

Something similar happened to the mathematical and physical sciences in western Europe in the seventeenth century; and in the following three hundred years the resulting reorganization of terms gave Europeans an advantage over other peoples whose traditional ways of describing the stars and other moving bodies were less accurate and explained fewer phenomena than those Galileo, Newton, and their fellow scientists had generated. In this case, Europe's superiority was intellectual. Anyone who learned to understand Newtonian physics and astronomy was ipso facto convinced that it was better than other modes of explanation. For a good many generations, technological improvements consonant with Newtonian science were only slenderly connected with theory; but as technical-theoretical connections multiplied, they provided another and very powerful argument for the superiority of European concepts.

The study of human society and of history has never mutated as sharply as the physical sciences did in seventeenth century Europe; and no one formulation of human relations (not even Aristotle's or Confucius') has ever commanded the sort of compelling intellectual force Newtonian astronomy commanded as against alternatives and predecessors in any and all parts of the earth. Human behavior, after all, is more complicated than that of pendulums, cannon balls, and planets. Emotions matter a great deal; and a very sensitive feedback affects any effort to describe human society. New insights tend to alter behavior, and altered behavior may (as it were arti-

1. Circularity of course prevails. One names what one notices and notices what one names. As knowledge becomes more abstract, it often happens that naming something new precedes its being observed.

ficially) either invalidate or confirm the insight. In either case, observed reality and the terms available for its analysis remain mutually dependent and very strongly culture-bound.

Yet, when the gap between observer and observed is unusually great, feedback may be slight. This can occur when an anthropologist from a western cultural metropolis studies a small, primitive community and learns the local language but does not reciprocate by teaching his to the natives. This minimizes the observer's active role in social process, though even here human interaction of course occurs. The alteration in behavior arising from the mere presence of a stranger, no matter how intent he may be on preserving pre-existing ways among those he is studying, must by definition remain beyond the stranger's observation. Nevertheless, it is surely real as anyone who has ever been observed while teaching a class or performing some other task will readily acknowledge. But whatever changes the anthropologist may precipitate by his presence remain slight as long as the people he observes do not try to understand and react to the terms and ideas with which he is seeking to make their behavior intelligible.

Other students of humanity move more or less in the same universe of discourse with those whose behavior they are seeking to understand. Consequently, the ideas and terms used by economists, political scientists, psychologists, sociologists, and other students of the human condition commonly do affect the behavior they attempt to describe on an ideational as well as on other levels. Human vanity being what it is, persons and groups whose points of view "catch on" in a larger environment are usually pleased rather than distressed by this phenomenon. They gladly become policy minded. Yet from a detached point of view, the task of analysis and understanding obviously becomes more difficult if the object of study keeps on changing in response to the observer's own intellectual efforts. Insofar as anthropologists are really able to observe without much altering what they study, they have the easier task.

Perhaps for this reason, the concepts I find most useful in trying to understand human history and social processes derive mainly from anthropology.

The basic notion is that of cultural pattern—a cluster of repeatable forms of behavior that complement one another in mutually supportive ways and give definition and a limited predictability to aspects of human conduct caught up in and conforming to such a pattern.

Patterns of behavior are sometimes conscious, and sometimes not. Conscious patterns we expect; men on the whole prefer to think that what they do and what they intend to do match up accurately. Thus school behavior is supposed to make young people literate, and usually does so. Far trickier are the aspects of social reality that produce patterns of which men are not conscious. The old fashioned alternation of economic boom and bust is an example of behavior which, prior to the development of a business cycle theory, created a pattern which was beyond the awareness of most of those affected by the phenomenon. A contemporary example may be in point: drivers caught in stop and go traffic on a crowded highway are seldom aware that their vehicles create a longitudinal wave pattern of alternating, equidistant nodes and antinodes that moves along the highway faster than the vehicles themselves. Yet in stop and go situations cars "condense" as they slow and "rarify" as they accelerate in a statistically regular fashion. The result is that the interaction of the physical constraints of the highway and of automobiles on the one hand and customary rules of driving on the other regularly produces a longitudinal wave, whether the drivers caught in the traffic jam are conscious of it or not.

The historian's task is to perceive both conscious and unconscious cultural patterns in the past behavior of men, and to notice how these patterns change through time. Until recently, most historians of Europe concentrated attention on patterns of behavior of which men in times past had been conscious. They assembled, criticized, and rendered coherent what dead men said about themselves and their predecessors. By eliminating bits of information that contradicted natural probability (as currently conceived), a credible and more or less connected story of public events across some thirty to forty centuries in a small (but as time went on expanding) segment of the earth's surface emerged from the concerted effort of innumerable scholars and historians. Their work created a richly figured carpet of fact and highly probable inference to which almost all reasonable men agree, once acquainted with the evidence. Weaving a few new threads into this magnificent handiwork was what scientific history meant to our nineteenth century predecessors.

The task continues indefinitely. Even if factual details to be filled in or corrected are liable to become less significant as time goes by, there are always new documents from relatively recent times freshly available for scholars to digest and fit into what had been known before. In addition, there were and continue to be areas of the earth for which the task of sifting, arranging, and making coherent the data recorded in surviving texts remains to be carried through. Obscure languages, difficult scripts, and other obstacles—geographical as well as bureaucratic—have often slowed but never stopped this tide of scholarship; and every so often, exploration of new texts turns up something that requires reconsideration of data derived from already familiar sources. This is currently true, for instance, in the field of Ottoman history, where the exploration of Turkish materials is only in a preliminary stage. When and if carried through with anything resembling the thoroughness with which Christian records have been exploited, Turkish sources will certainly require some important readjustments of received views about the history of southeastern Europe, especially between 1350 and 1750.

Yet this critical editorial process is only a part of what historians really do. Besides editing what men of past ages had to say about themselves, historians have always also looked for aspects of the human past of which men of the times were not themselves aware. Such matters are by definition not directly attested in surviving documents, but, with suitable ingenuity, can often be read between the lines. Yet when the work of the historian consists largely of declaring or merely assuming that men were doing things of which they were quite unconscious, the range for fantasy and possible error enormously enlarges. Such risks are counterbalanced by what at least seems like the possibility of penetrating beneath appearances to underlying causes and conditions of human experience. Historians who refuse to say anything not directly attested in the written records that happen to have survived from some past time (and there are some who claim to do this) simply close themselves off from trying to understand more and differently than men of old were capable of.

The question remains: how can one control fantasy? In recognizing a pattern in the past, the observer is at least as important as the observed. An historian is, indeed, very like an anthropologist in the sense that men long dead cannot alter their affairs any more than a primitive people can respond to the concepts an anthropologist applies to the analysis of their behavior. Yet any advantage that this may create is more than counterbalanced by the haphazard way in which records from the past have been preserved, so that all too often the data an historian most wants in order to test his hypothesis are not readily available and may not be available at all.

Moreover, there are two other complications. First of all, different patterns may inhere in the same reality, and there is always an appropriate scale to be used for the perception of each kind of pattern. Thus electrons, atoms, and molecules along with cells, trees, and a forest may coexist in the same physical structures without any contradiction; but quite different scales of observation and analytical constructs are needed to recognize any one of them. Second, over time and across space men's analytical constructs evolve differently. No one, aware of this, can believe that patterns he happens to find convincing, living in the United States in the second half of the twentieth century, will satisfy all his contemporaries, far less future generations.

Appeal to observation as a test of truth will not usually settle very much, because what one sees, whether in a landscape or in the immensely tangled and diverse record of the past, depends so intimately on what one is looking for; and that in turn depends on a matrix of key terms that direct attention and guide inquiry. Perhaps an example will point this up. I recently had occasion to fly from Vienna to Athens, and spent an absorbed half-hour looking out the window and watching for the shift from long acre field shapes, such as those prevailing around Vienna, to the pattern of square and irregularly shaped fields that set in north of Skoplje. Probably no one else in that plane noticed what I saw; and I saw what I did only because I had read what Marc Bloch has to say about field shapes in medieval France, and knew that a boundary between two styles of cultivation—one north European, and one Mediterranean—must exist along the route my plane was taking. The "fact" was there for anyone to notice; but given the immense actual variety of field shapes, and the innumerable other things a man's eye might look at in the landscape unrolling below, it was only by virtue of a pre-existing pattern of expectation that I was able to filter out irrelevancies in order to recognize, with a thrill of satisfaction, the point at which the two types of field shape began to intermingle and then watch the long acre swiftly disappear—for the line is, in fact, quite sharp.

Satisfactory cases of historical discovery are of this sort: when a clear and distinct expectation meets unmistakable and relatively simple confirmation with data which any reasonable man will confirm if his attention is called to the matter. Not infrequently, however, the best available hypothesis is such that not all reasonable men find it persuasive, even if the facts and their proposed interpretation have been brought fully to everyone's attention. The result is debate and disagreement, often without decisive resolution. Such controversy may remain cool and academic; it may, however, enter the arena of public affairs and arouse intense, even explosive, emotions. The fanaticisms of persecutors and heretics, that bulk so large in the human record, show how firmly beliefs about history and society are often held.

The fact is that men cannot refrain from embracing controversial and imperfectly convincing hypotheses. To act upon and react to the world requires us to organize what lies around us comprehensibly, that is, to filter out meaningless detail and background "noise" in order to be free to attend to what does matter, that is, what does, quite literally, make sense. And if what makes sense to some seems merest myth to others, this does not prevent groups of men from acting as if their chosen or inherited ideas about human affairs were true and righteous altogether. Anyone who challenges such behavior will be resented and may provoke persecution if what he challenges seems sufficiently important to those defending their version of the truth.

Yet views do change. What is sacred and indefeasible to one

generation becomes marginal or even completely unimportant to their successors over long enough periods of time. And the evolution of men's views of themselves and of the societies around them (as well as of the physical world) surely exhibits more than random whim or a succession of idle intellectual fashions. Evidence and logic as well as the pragmatic test of what does in fact conduce to survival affect the ideas and beliefs men hold. Errors tend to disappear, if by error we mean ideas that frequently lead to disappointment or disaster. Conversely, truths that instruct men to behave in ways that often bring satisfaction and that conduce to a closer coincidence between expectation and what actually occurs seem likely to endure and even to spread across time and space.

Historians' efforts to describe the past and analyze what mattered in that past constitute an important part of the European and Western effort to revise and correct prevailing understanding of public affairs. This, in fact, is the main claim the historical profession has on the indulgence of modern society.

By assessing and reassessing the past, historians offer directly or by implication alternative understandings of the present. Amongst these, others may choose. In choosing they enter actively into the vast evolutionary process through which all dimensions of human culture respond to experience and through hit and miss more than by logic and prescience improve the accuracy and adequacy of human responses to the human (as well as to the natural) environment.

Since no one can abstract himself from this historic process, any would-be historian (or any other intellectually ambitious person) must simply do the best he can with the state of the art he inherits. Everyone everywhere is caught up in an inescapable circularity between expectation (defined by available terms and their interrelations) and experience. Each affects the other always, but of the two, expectation plays the organizing, dominating role. It is subject to correction more through friction with other abstract classificatory systems of expectation than by observable recalcitrance of experience per se. All actual expectation systems do in fact organize experience successfully, thanks to the human capacity for not attending to trivial background noise. No conceivable system of expectation could exhaust all potential data, explain everything, and give meaning and importance to every accessible input. Indeed, the whole purpose and practical function of abstraction, stored up ahead of time in a pattern of expectation, is to allow us to attend only to the meaningful fraction of potential stimuli, while neglecting everything else—fly specks on the manuscript page, dust smells in the library, miracles attested by two independent witnesses, and all the rest.

The only appropriate posture, in view of these considerations, seems to be a suitably bold tentativeness, recognizing how fragile as well as how powerful language is in organizing experience, aware also of how every conceptual scheme, our own included, is an historical product, subject to further evolution —or to becoming a dead end, a mere antiquarian curiosity. In such a spirit, then, let me sketch in the abstract the expectations that govern my approach to history before attempting to apply the scheme to European history in subsequent chapters.

Patterns of culture—repeatable behavior recognizable in the lives of relatively large numbers of men, often millions or hundreds of millions—are the entities that concern me. Such a pattern is recognized by an intuitive leap, generalizing from a limited body of information; and the primary test of such a concept is how well it can accommodate additional information that had not yet been encountered at the time the intuitive leap was made.

Patterns of culture interact whenever men who share a given pattern of culture encounter strangers who do not share it. The strangers of course have their own set of culture patterns so that the encounter is an encounter of two different cultural patterns imprinted upon the partners to the encounter. In such cases mutual repulsion with no important change on either side is probably the commonest response. Sometimes, however, one or other partner to the encounter recognizes something attractive in the other's attainments, or something so formidable that steps must be taken to improve his own defenses lest some future collision bring disaster.

Encounters of this sort, therefore, provoke men to alter, adjust, improve their particular cultural inheritance. Recombination of familiar elements to invent something new is one possibility. A second and far more common response to perceived deficiency in one's own cultural inheritance is to attempt to borrow and adjust whatever it was in the stranger's cultural accouterments that seemed superior. Through most of man's time on earth, human groups probably met strangers whose culture differed from their own within only a limited range. Hunters meeting hunters, and subsistence agriculturalists encountering subsistence agriculturalists were in a good position to appraise anything new in the strangers' repertory of skills and could borrow whatever seemed advantageous with little difficulty.

But there are circumstances, and have been ever since agriculture first became a basic economic support and way of life for entire human communities, in which strangers encounter one another as bearers of fundamentally different styles of life. In such cases, borrowing is more difficult. If it goes beyond trade for gewgaws and trifles, the effort to appropriate some strange new skill may create far-reaching conflicts between old and new cultural patterns. One change may lead to others, so that within a relatively short period of time the recipient society may find itself compelled to a kind of cultural mutation.

Across still wider cultural gaps, as when hunters and gatherers encounter civilized societies, not infrequently the upshot is disruption and dissolution of the weaker society. For hunters and gatherers brought into contact with civilized ways are likely to become bewildered and demoralized, trying vainly to cope with what they have to admit, even to themselves, is a style of life superior to what they had themselves inherited. Short of dissolution, weaker societies can sometimes come to terms with a more powerful neighbor by submitting to various forms of subordination: paying taxes and rents, performing labor services on demand, or the like. Withdrawal to some refuge area where geographical obstacles prevent the powerful strangers from impinging is another possibility and in fact all surviving examples of hunting and gathering societies that remain for modern anthropologists to study took this path.[2]

Cultural patterns that are able to withstand comparison with those of strangers successfully tend to cluster at places where contacts among men of diverse cultural backgrounds are frequent. This is so because in such locations men have more choices thrust upon them; and having choices tend to prefer

2. This, in turn, means that inferences about the cultural character and especially the psychological attitudes of early human communities based on projecting backward in time the fearful and withdrawn behavior of contemporary hunters and gatherers is misleading. When all men were hunters, and better hunters than any of their animal rivals, timidity in meeting strangers or fear of unfamiliar places, and so forth, probably played a far smaller role than it does among surviving hunters, who have retained their style of culture only by systematically retreating from disturbing contacts with outsiders.

ways that seem in some sense superior [3] to available alternatives.

These exposed locations were established through interactions between geographical layout and the technology of transport and communications. Geography channeled patterns of transport and communication toward certain nodes where culturally fertile encounters consequently became more frequent. In addition, some landscapes were especially hospitable to diverse occupational exploitation, permitting hunters, herders, and agriculturalists to exist in close proximity with one another, for instance. Such diversity also provoked interaction and innovation at a pace that utterly outstripped anything that had occurred among the undifferentiated hunting communities within which our earliest human ancestors lived.

3. This is a loaded word. Romantics and other rebels against the complexities and perplexities of civilized life are prone to repudiate the assertion that civilized ways are superior to primitive and simpler patterns of human life. Obviously, everything depends on what one judges important, valuable, worth having. All I intend by the term is a description of men's real choices in adopting some ways of behavior and rejecting others they judged less attractive, that is, inferior. In using such terms I do not mean to imply my own personal endorsement of the wisdom of actual choices, though in fact, being a man, most of the choices men have in fact made commend themselves also to me. Thus, wealth and power seem preferable to poverty and impotence, to me and to most men. Choices aimed at these goals usually prevailed. Beauty and logical consistency are also powerful and widespread desiderata that often influenced real human choices.

Conflicting values, of course, exist and mistaken decisions are common. In particular, human life is haunted by persistent tension between long-run and short-run payoffs. But in the aggregate, if relevant statistics could be discovered, they would probably show that long-run payoffs with respect to individual life spans (though short-run socially and geologically) tend to prevail. Such at any rate were the sort of choices enjoined by all the traditional moral codes which civilized mankind inherits. The positive survival value of such codes for individuals and for society at large seems as unquestionable as is the remarkable way in which all the important moral systems of civilized mankind converge in practice toward what Christians know as the Golden Rule.

Places where men had maximal chance to choose the more effective, more impressive, more attractive way of doing things thus came into existence. The result was to create clusters of superior skill; and these clusters constituted the early centers of civilization.

As such centers defined themselves, complex and continuing interaction between civilized center and the barbarian fringes round about set in. Barbarian is here intended as a corollary of the term "civilized." Barbarians are peoples in touch with a civilized community, aware of the superiority of civilized accomplishments, yet also attached to their own different and distinctive ways. Ambivalence results, mingling envy with disdain; but there is a persistent strain among barbarians to appropriate and make their own at least some aspects of the civilized cluster of skills as a way to improve their own lot and escape from a nagging sense of inferiority vis-à-vis their civilized contemporaries.

The upshot of such interaction was an outflow of culture traits from the civilized center to neighbors and neighbors' neighbors. Such flows sometimes traversed considerable distances when the borrowed item was easy to transport and could be smoothly insinuated into the receiving culture patterns of many differing peoples. In other cases geographical or cultural obstacles prevented the spread of a technique or idea for centuries despite proximity and ample opportunity for one community to learn from another.

The circumstances that lead to particular decisions to borrow or to accept an innovation generated by local reaction to alien contact vary greatly, and in most cases details are irrecoverable. Irrational as well as rational factors operate in human responses to novelty. All the same, acceptance of change is not wholly random nor is it uniformly distributed in time and space. Clearly, where multiple cultural models are available, departures from old ways become more probable; and after a particular society has opted for a series of alterations in accustomed patterns of behavior, resistance to further departures from tradition weakens—at least up to a point at which the entire psychological structure of meanings and values with which people are used to reacting to the world around them threatens to fall apart. At that point, resistance to further change may suddenly intensify. Various sorts of frantic behavior may arise until the crisis passes as new habits for coping with the world establish themselves. Alternatively, the bearers of an endangered cultural tradition may die off, or survive biologically but disappear as a separate cultural entity by dissolving into some adjacent or circumambient social and cultural structure.

Within a complex civilized society, sects and occupational or other groups may withdraw at least in part, deliberately rejecting elements in the dominant culture and substituting norms of their own. The possibility of such pluralism also allows initially independent barbarian cultures to be absorbed into a civilized body politic, becoming like a sect with ways adjusted to symbiosis with the larger society but differing from its norms in various important aspects. Diversity thus incorporated within civilized communities is likely to promote cultural innovation, at least until a generally satisfactory accommodation among diverse groups somehow arises; whereupon fresh contacts with new kinds of strangers, as communications nets alter and expand, are liable to start the entire process of mutual adjustment and readjustment, internal as well as external, all over again.

When the internal complexity of a civilized society becomes great enough, with enough internal friction points and interfaces, a self-sustaining reaction may perhaps set in, provoking an accelerating pace of social change as one internally generated change provokes several others, and they in their turn provoke still others, ad infinitum. Yet in the absence of renewed external challenges, it is not clear that even the most rapid and far-reaching alterations of human society will not in time settle back toward equilibrium. Simple, small societies surely tend toward stable equilibrium; civilizations have not yet been around long enough (a mere 5000 years after all) for a civilized equilibrium to define itself, though various periods in Europe's civilized career and more notably in China's approached the ideal of stability.

Behind all social change must ultimately lie moments of human creativity. No one, I think, has developed a really satisfactory theory to explain this rare and exceptional sort of behavior. Individual genius as well as conditions of social receptivity to and provocation of individual acts of creative innovation remain mysterious. It seems clear, nevertheless, that innovation originates in individual minds, though in most cases a circle of kindred spirits, sharing common concerns and debating or experimenting with common problems, provides a necessary and indispensable stimulus to the individual inventor. Even sour and isolated genius draws sustenance for its creativity from the environment—perhaps by books more than by word of mouth, or from other impersonal forms of encounter.

I suspect that creativity is also always an affair of sudden intuitive insight when familiar bits and pieces of experience rearrange themselves in the mind's eye suggesting some new relationship, some new possibility, some new meaning that no one has ever seen before. Sometimes, perhaps usually, such experiences lead nowhere; most new ideas like most biological mutations are bad ones. But occasionally the innovator can convince a public of the truth, beauty, or utility of his insight and thus alter behavior in wider and wider circles, as the innovation proves itself in the lives of dozens, hundreds, thousands, and ultimately sometimes in the lives of millions of others.

The processes whereby a new invention propagates itself within a society are almost identical with the processes whereby borrowed innovation resulting from contact with an alien society is propagated. Yet there is this difference. Men who accept and propagate a brand-new discovery or invention have the weight of tradition against them. They are not spurred to act by fear or envy of some potent foreigner who seems superior in some important ways. Until recently, the result was inhibitory. If the innovation has not been thought of or needed by ancestors, most men judged that it could not be very valuable. With no outside threat to spur acceptance of change, conservative rejection was the normal reaction.

Nonetheless, men do play about with familiar elements of their world and every so often hit upon some recombination that because it seems an improvement on what had been done or known before does attract adherents. Technological improvements that allow better results with less effort are perhaps easiest to recognize; but logical and aesthetic improvements may also command relatively broad recognition, at least in some circumstances. Here the rule of compound interest applies: societies that have already accepted important changes within living memory are likely to provoke invention. This is so because past change creates new possibilities and, usually, also creates discrepancies that acute minds may notice and seek to repair. Such societies, likewise, are less prone to resist additional changes, since the same social circumstances that encourage invention by the few also facilitate its acceptance by the many.

As a result, successful innovations tend to cluster in time and space. When this happens, what I propose to call a "metropolitan center" asserts itself. Such innovations by definition prove widely influential and acceptable to large numbers of people; this requires geographical spread from the locus of their initial emergence. When a number of such diffusion processes are simultaneously in train, what may be called a "cultural slope" arises, descending with varying gradients from the peak at the metropolitan center as one travels further and further away among peoples and communities where only some and eventually little or no trace of reaction to the achievements of the metropolitan center can be detected.

This is really no more than a metaphor, summing up millions and sometimes millions upon millions of individual reactions to personal experience. Moreover, the geological metaphor of peak and slope is imperfect, for in the same space-time quite different peaks and slopes may coexist, depending on what aspects of cultural behavior one thinks of. Thus, for instance, in Europe, 1650–1700, a map of metropolitan center and cultural slopes for music would differ sharply from that for physics; and still different patterns would exist for such things as mining technology, agricultural improvement, military organization, belles lettres, or for the writing and study of history. Moreover, during the last hundred years, when instantaneous communications have reached around the globe, a number of professional skills have arisen whose exercise is not closely tied to any single geographical center. Among experts like atomic-physicists or radio astronomers, reaction time to any important innovation, regardless of where it starts from is now very brief indeed.

In these conditions the metaphor of metropolitan center and cultural slope loses most of its relevance. But in earlier ages, when communications were much slower and resistance to innovation tended to be greater, there was a definite tendency for major innovation to flourish within quite limited geographical loci, and, characteristically, to persist for only limited periods of time. Major innovation of one sort tended to occur in association with innovations in other sorts of activity producing what later generations often recognized as a "Golden Age," when important and enduring new things were discovered, expressed, or acted upon for the first time.

To be caught up in the midst of such an age was not very pleasant: too many things became uncertain, too many anxieties were let loose. After all, really important innovation is to be expected only when men recognize some deficiency and lack in what they already know or do, and the most poignant way to recognize such deficiency is to feel hurt or deprived, whether in body or mind or both. Golden ages glitter only in retrospect; anxiety, even anguish, is the more characteristic contemporary experience.

Yet no age is correctly characterized by any single state of mind. Any society and every age exhibits a wide gamut of temperaments; and within an individual life, youth is normally more sanguine and eager for change than old age. Moreover, there are times when innovation commends itself to a majority. Times when some decisive act of daring or the discovery of some new technique has unlocked new sources of wealth are likely to have this character, since almost all men approve of increased wealth. We happen to live in such an age and therefore take change for granted. But in human history as a whole, such periods are very rare, though likely to be important. The normal condition of human society is near to stable equilibrium, at least when measured against the span of individual human life. This, surely, was the way the world was for our hunting and gathering ancestors; and inherited human aptitudes in all probability makes us yearn for such stability.

Civilization, and the restless changeability associated with complex, unstable societies, may be viewed, indeed, as a kind of cancerous growth; the result of unusual stresses overthrowing the normal restraints and self-regulating controls that kept precivilized human communities within familiar, customary, and habitual lines. An overwhelming majority of humankind, I think, is always trying to regain this lost ancestral Eden. Men do so by attempting to weave around themselves a comfortable cocoon of habits that work, that is, habits that produce wanted and wonted results. If enough individuals succeed, then of course the society to which they belong must also achieve near-stability. It is the failure of this effort that promotes change. Individual failure to find a set of habits that satisfies needs and expectations adequately becomes en masse a failure of society to achieve stability.

I want to emphasize how recalcitrant humankind is to the uncertainty and changeability of civilized life because in most of what follows, social innovation will almost monopolize attention, and it might be supposed that because I write admiringly about those who pioneered new patterns of thought and conduct I believe that the attractions of civilization are self-evident, and that rational choice would always dictate preference for civilized as against simpler styles of life. The matter is, in a sense, the reverse; those who willingly chose civilization did so, usually, by grasping for some of the technical and intellectual and artistic power civilized patterns of behavior create, but did so without being fully aware of the costs involved.

Among these costs were uncertainty and anxiety, arising from incapacity to forecast what the consequences of particular kinds of behavior will be. Insofar as real civilized societies succeed in minimizing these costs, it is by creating a broad array of institutions within whose framework consequences of behavior are more nearly predictable. Insofar as individuals can identify themselves with some institution, then it becomes possible to discharge anxiety by assuming and asserting an identity between the person—poor, frustrated, helpless though he may be—and the grander collective entity-nation, race, church, sect, corporation, street gang, or whatever else. But with an irony that constantly recurs in social affairs, the cost of security attained by personal identification with some larger institution or group is also real; for conflicts among such organized entities can become more destructive and dangerous than individual conflicts ever are. War between sovereign states is the chief but by no means the sole example of this phenomenon. Attaining stable and satisfactory adjustment among institutions is about as difficult as attaining stable and satisfactory adjustments among individuals. It can be done; simple isolated societies regularly succeed. But civilized societies have only occasionally shown signs of settling down toward some more or less stable modus vivendi among institutions before fresh disturbance from within or without sets in.

However strongly humankind is predisposed to prefer stability and predictability to chaos and uncertainty—and I think it difficult to exaggerate our preference for situations we know how to cope with successfully by summoning an appropriate habit into action—all the same it would be lopsided and misleading not to recognize the reality of positive human impulses toward novelty and adventure. Curiosity is widespread. Impulses to take risks, face the unknown, escape from habitual routines are also real, especially when prevailing routines do not provide adequate scope for the full range of human penchants and abilities, as is sometimes clearly the case.

Once physiological needs are met, if time and energy remain, playfulness asserts itself. This may find muscular expression in sports and dancing; it may find verbal expression in telling stories, jokes, myths. This little essay along with all other historical writing, partakes of the character of verbal word play, elaborating upon the past. There are genuine satisfactions in seeing a new pattern of relationships suddenly leap into view as one mulls over familiar information; similarly, an artist, or performer, takes satisfaction in successful elaboration or renewed demonstration of his skill. To be sure, it is sometimes hard to separate intrinsic gratifications from the praise bestowed on performers who conform closely enough to public expectation to earn praise; but thinkers and artists experience a long enough time between the moment of conception and its public presentation that there can be no doubt of the reality of both joys—that of personal and private discovery, and that of its public appreciation.

Deliberate and playful elaboration of skills and concepts finds greatly enlarged scope whenever a circle of experts arises among whom admiration and applause is accorded to anyone who thinks or does something better than ever before. But systematically innovative professional circles have been few and short-lived in civilized history. Successes tend to be ritualized and rendered at least semisacred by repetition and the awe-filled admiration of later generations. In other words, the conservative, normative penchant of humankind at large was more than sufficient to contain and safely encapsulate professionalized innovation, at least until very recent times. Even the massive contemporary unleashing of professionalized innovation may yet be contained; though probably not until several human lifetimes have passed.

I conclude, therefore, that through the larger part of recorded history the main drive wheel of historical change was contacts among strangers, causing men on both sides of such encounters to reconsider and in some cases to alter their familiar ways of behaving. Such contacts and the reactions to them generated civilizations. Within such civilizations, like a volcano in eruption, there arose specially active "metropolitan centers" of innovation. The emergence of such centers in turn created cultural slopes. From time to time metropolitan centers shifted location, or a quite new center asserted itself; with such changes came changes in direction and velocity of cultural flows, that is, alterations in the alignment of cultural slopes. Such alterations, in turn, may be taken as defining major periods or eras of history.

Armed with these notions about historical method and social process, it now remains to apply them to the data of European history, in the hope that a plausible and intelligible overall pattern may result.

III

EUROPE TO A.D. 900

The school book definition of the European continent, divided from Asia by the Ural Mountains and an imaginary line extending southward to the Caspian and thence to the Black Sea along the crest of the Caucasus Mountain Range, bears little relation to the usual historical identification of Europe with a style of life that in recent times centered upon France, England, the Low Countries, and parts of Italy and Germany. In the first Christian centuries, the discrepancy between cultural and geographical definitions of "Europe" was particularly wide; for the Roman empire, in embracing all the shores of the Mediterranean touched three continents; yet Roman history is usually regarded as part of the history of Europe.

Like so much else, our concept of "Europe" contrasted with Asia and Africa descends from ancient Greece. Early Hellenic seamen located Asia on the eastern side of one of the most easily traveled seas of the earth—the Aegean; and located Africa to the south of an only slightly more difficult traverse between Crete and Egypt-Libya. Yet the terms stuck, largely because the cultural configurations of the time gave "Asia" and "Africa," thus defined, a palpable reality. Moreover, the Asian and African strangers Greek seamen encountered were capable of challenging Greek autonomy, as the invasion of Xerxes' armies and Herodotus' awe at the attainments of the sophisticated Egyptians clearly showed. The effort to use the Urals and Caucasus as boundary lines came much later, though still within classical times, as a way of lending precision to what by then had become a fixed habit of thought among Greeks and those influenced by them.

This evolution of geographical terms points to an important fact of human geography. Distant and culturally alien lands like "Asia" and "Africa" were named by Greek seamen because their ships took them there. Travel overland was far more difficult and when it came to carrying goods, costly since pack animals had to be fed, whereas a sailing ship, once put together, derived its movement from the boundless air. Road building, of course, allowed wheeled vehicles to travel cross country, and this speeded overland transport greatly; but the construction and maintenance of roads passable for wagons was very costly. In ancient times, only well-administered states, like the Roman empire in its prime or the empires of Assyria and of Persia before it, were able to maintain a road network of more than local scope.

The military advantage attainable by quicker marching toward a threatened point obviously justified coercive concentration of labor for road building in the eyes of Assyrian, Persian, and Roman rulers, and incidentally made the cross country movement of goods cheaper and easier. Yet even the best roads could not carry goods as rapidly and cheaply as ships could. As a result, cities that could not be reached by shipping remained small and comparatively unimportant. Under the conditions of transport prevailing until the mid-nineteenth century, when railroads began to change things, water transport was so much superior to transport overland that large concentrations of men who did not produce their own food by their own muscular effort could flourish only close to navigable water. Waterways, therefore, remained until very recently the major determinants of where cities and civilizations arose.

Europe's configuration divides the continent into a southern or Mediterranean zone and a northern or Atlantic zone, depending on which way navigable streams run. Despite several important military incursions from the north, until about 1600, the Mediterranean zone of Europe remained culturally dominant; since that date the Atlantic zone surpassed the more ancient centers of the south in most respects. This is probably the most important watershed in European history, though 400 years of Atlantic dominance is a small segment of time to set against the 4000 years during which the Mediterranean zone of Europe was culturally ahead of the north.

Mediterranean primacy rested on historical circumstance. The earliest European civilized societies were domiciled around the shores of the Aegean. Subsequent ages inherited skills and techniques which, elaborated over time, sustained comparatively vast concentrations of wealth and population at varying locations within the Mediterranean zone from the beginnings of Minoan civilization in Crete (ca. 2100 B.C.) until the present. On this basis, civilized societies arose and flourished along the northern coastlands of the Mediterranean uninterruptedly. No other part of the European continent enjoyed such an inheritance, and to overtake and surpass the achievements of the men of the south was not easy, given the severer climate and initial technical handicaps under which northern peoples labored.

These technical differentials between north and south constituted a second basis for Mediterranean primacy. They were fundamentally twofold: agricultural in the first place, nautical in the second. The agricultural superiority of Mediterranean lands over northerly ones lasted only until A.D. 900 or thereabouts; hence this chapter breaks off at the point in time when one of the important bases of Mediterranean primacy disappeared. The nautical superiority of the Mediterranean lasted longer, for, despite the Vikings' daring, it was only shortly before 1500 that improvements in ship design and navigation began to make travel on the stormy and tide-troubled Atlantic waters almost as safe as seafaring within the Mediterranean. As this was achieved, northern-built ships came to enjoy a clear superiority to less stoutly constructed Mediterranean vessels, and the second technical basis of Mediterranean cultural primacy dissolved. Within about a century, Atlantic Europe was then in a position to overcome its age-old deficiencies vis-à-vis the south, and in due season, soon after 1600, took over cultural leadership of the continent as a whole.

Throughout premodern times, the steppe lands of the Ukraine, Rumania, and Hungary constituted a different kind of sea—a sea of grass—across which horse nomads traveled with an ease and speed rivaling that of seamen. Nomads ordinarily could not conveniently carry large, bulky goods; they often preferred rapine and raiding to more peaceful encounters, since their superior mobility gave them persistent advantages in military confrontations with settled, agricultural folk. On occasion, however, when civilized defenses made raiding costly, nomads fell back on more peaceable trading. Their abundant animals made it comparatively easy for them to organize pack trains capable of carrying goods of high value in proportion to their bulk for very long distances. Accordingly, beginning in the first century B.C. caravans moved across the interior deserts and open grasslands of Eurasia, all the way from China to Syria. Alternative routes debouched on the Black Sea via Trebizond or the Crimea or reached river ports on the Vistula and Niemen.

The horse nomads of the steppes checked agricultural exploitation of the fertile Ukrainian grasslands for many centuries. Not until after 1600, when hand guns transformed the age-old military balance between agricultural and nomad communities, did the steppes of southeastern Europe really open up for pioneer settlement, although in earlier ages there had been several periods during which relatively peaceful conditions permitted cultivators to extend their fields into the grasslands on significant, though never on a decisive, scale. Such advances of agriculture were subsequently rolled back, when new and more ruthless raiders arrived from the east, ravaging farmsteads, slaughtering or enslaving whomever they could catch, and driving survivors to take refuge in the forests of the north or in the Carpathian and other mountain zones lying south and west.

The soil and climate of the forested zone of eastern Europe made agriculture a less rewarding occupation than it was in the more westerly parts of the continent, where a longer growing season and richer soils allowed a better return on seed than was to be expected in the northeast. The marginal character of cereal cultivation in Sweden, Poland, and Russia,[1] combined with the exposure of the more fertile parts of the two latter lands to nomads raiding from the steppes, meant that only slender populations, dependent in part on hunting and gathering from the forests, could survive in most of these regions, at least as long as the peoples of the steppelands remained a threat.

Yet the vast reaches of Russian rivers, easily navigable for hundreds or even thousands of miles, made it possible to gather trade goods—furs, wax, honey, slaves, amber—across

1. Seed to harvest ratios of 1:2 and 1:3 were more or less normal; in a bad year total loss, or a harvest only a little larger than the seed that had been planted, was to be expected. By contrast seed to harvest ratio of 1:10 were possible and 1:4 or 1:5 were common in western Europe. Cf. the very instructive data gathered in Slicher van Bath, "Yield Ratios, 810–1820," *Afdeeling Agarische Geschiedenis Landbouwhogeschool* (Wageningen, 1963), No. 10.

comparatively long distances. Beginning in the tenth century, the same arterial system allowed state building on a territorially vast scale despite the sparse and impoverished condition of the population. Rivers, in short, did for northeastern Europe what seas did for the south—that is, they provided a means for easy transport across long distances. Northwestern Europe had the best of both worlds, enjoying access to a fine natural network of navigable riverways debouching into a number of narrow and at least relatively protected seas: the Baltic, the North Sea, and the English Channel. Yet this advantage remained only potential until movement by sea could attain routine regularity. In a similar fashion, the full potential of the Russian river system could not develop without free movement across the sea of grass lying to the south. The struggle of Russian agriculturalists and rivermen to stave off or overcome the horsemen of the steppe was analogous to the problem northwestern Europe faced in trying to tame the pirates and master the tides and storms of Atlantic waters. Both aimed at breaking through a persistent barrier to movement of men and goods, and neither succeeded until after A.D. 900 in more than sporadic and temporary fashion.

The Mediterranean zone lacked large navigable rivers, with the conspicuous exceptions of the Nile, the Po, and the rivers debouching into the Black Sea. As long as their horses sustained their military dominance, the nomads of the steppe deprived the Black Sea rivers of most of their potential significance. But the Nile from deep antiquity and the Po from A.D. 900 provided a basis for local and markedly individualized styles of civilization that stand somewhat apart from the cultural history of the rest of the Mediterranean. That history turned on movement across open water, whether the Mediterranean proper or its connecting seas—the Black, the Aegean, and the Adriatic. Navigation in these waters required far less skill than was needed amidst the storms and tides of the

Atlantic and its connecting seas. Yet the storms which do afflict the Mediterranean during winter months were more than ships and mariners of Greek and Roman times cared to confront, and with good reason, as the Bible story of St. Paul's shipwreck may remind us. Indeed, in ancient times, it was customary to haul ships ashore in winter and sail only during the season of the year when the trades, blowing steadily from the northeast under constantly clear skies, made navigation easy. Since grain harvest fell in May or June and good sailing weather lasted until about October, this allowed enough time to carry grain supplies to whatever capital city or cities dominated Mediterranean shores. This essential attended to, movements of other goods and of men could and did accommodate to the seasonal pattern of Mediterranean shipping without much difficulty.

Capacity to concentrate enough grain to support scores of thousands of city folk who did not raise their own food was an important prerequisite for developing the kind of cultures in the Mediterranean zone that were capable of commanding admiration and inspiring imitation elsewhere in Europe. This required not only ships and sailors, but a hinterland whose inhabitants were either compelled or induced to produce and part with a surplus of grain and other commodities. This prerequisite for all premodern civilizations was achieved sometimes by force, sometimes by offering goods produced in civilized workshops in exchange. In most situations both elements were present; and both trade and compulsion often achieved a customary definition that softened and disguised the collision of interests involved.

Characteristically, rents and taxes were collected by force or threat of force. Local magnates usually collected small surpluses locally, playing the role of landlord, and then exchanged part of what they had thus accumulated for luxury goods brought from afar. Such civilized luxuries were offered for sale by seafaring merchants whose numerical weakness vis-à-vis local populations made forcible seizure of desired local commodities—grain, metals, lumber—impracticable. This sort of symbiosis between a local landlord class and civilized merchants and traders was necessary to allow smooth concentration of food and other raw materials at the center. Local landlords, in turn, glimpsing the refinements and luxuries of civilized life, became barbarians par excellence: aware of what was possible and aware, also, of their own inability to rival locally the products and skills of full blown urban civilization.

In ancient times, the Mediterranean urban centers had more than fine cloth and trinkets with which to charm the barbarians of the European hinterland. Olive oil and wine served as civilized staple exports. These were commodities requiring some capital, for a first crop could be produced only after several years of waiting for the trees and vines to begin to bear fruit. In addition, olive trees will not survive severe or prolonged frost. This set sharp limits on their habitat even within Mediterranean lands. Some skill and fairly elaborate machinery is also needed to produce wine and oil from the fruit as it comes from the vines and trees. Yet once the uses of wine and of oil became familiar, landlords and chieftains of the backwoods areas of the ancient Mediterranean, wherever they lived, were willing, indeed eager, to exchange grain and other products of their fields and forests for the precious wine and oil.

Terms of this trade favored the civilized center. The produce of an acre of land planted with vines or olive trees could usually be exchanged for a quantity of grain that required far more ground for its growth. This made it practicable to concentrate relatively large amounts of food and raw materials in places where wine and oil was available for export. In effect, the pattern of trade enlisted the active cooperation of thousands of distant landlords in the delicate and difficult task of squeezing unrequited goods and services from the peasantry. Only after local magnates had collected a quantity of goods in demand at the civilized center, could they hope to exchange such goods for the wine and oil they came to prize so highly.

In the earliest stages of Mediterranean civilized history this pattern of exchange was of central importance. Crete appears to have been the first great center of both wine and oil export; the wealth of Minoan palaces probably depended upon exchange of these two commodities for metals, grain, and whatever else the lords of Knossos required or took delight in bringing to their courts. Similar exchanges may also have helped sustain the might of Mycenae, although there can be no doubt that direct resort to force—the plundering of distant coasts and sacking of cities as celebrated by Homer—played a much larger role in Mycenaean economics than had been the case in Minoan times.

We are much better informed about classical Greece, where first Ionia and then Attica, rose to prosperity and mercantile pre-eminence with the help of massive oil and wine exports. To be sure, Athens in its most glorious days supplemented income from trade with tribute monies collected from subject cities all round the Aegean; but many of these tribute paying communities, in their turn, derived the means wherewith to pay the assessed tribute by exporting wine and oil.

In the fifth century B.C., market production of wine and oil was still quite new and was restricted to the Aegean area for the most part. Yet Greek vessels made these products available throughout the Mediterranean coastlands. Response among Scyths, Thracians, Macedonians, Illyrians, Italians, and other barbarians was tremendous. In later times terms of trade within the Mediterranean regions never favored oil and wine producers so strongly. It was never afterward possible to exercise such an easy economic preponderance as Athens enjoyed from 470 to 431 B.C. without resort to rents, taxes, and tributes on a far larger scale than anything Pericles or even Cleon conceived of.

The special quality of Athenian culture in its Golden Age, when custom lost its hold and everything had to be examined and considered afresh, was deeply tinctured by this unique geo-economic balance between an oil-wine export metropolis and a hinterland eager to accept all that the Athenians and their fellow Greeks cared to spare from their own consumption of these commodities. In particular, the equal participation of citizen farmers in the affairs of the Athenian polis was sustained by the active role these same farmers had in the production and marketing of the wine and oil whose export, more than anything else, sustained the entire Athenian economy. City folk could not afford to scorn and deride those whose land and labor provided such a vital link in the city's prosperity; still less could they neglect the armed and organized might of these same stalwart farmers, concentrated in the city's phalanx. In this fashion, a firm bond between urban and rural segments of the Athenian citizenry could be maintained. The agricultural producers of Attica, instead of sinking to the level of an excluded and oppressed peasantry (as seemed to be happening before Peisistratus [d. 527 B.C.] organized production of wine and oil for export) instead came to embody the very essence of the Greek ideal. The Athenian farmers were free men, each the master of himself and his land, head of his family and household, and an autonomous participant in public affairs, with the right to vote on all important matters of policy.

Lest we idealize Greek democracy unduly, it is worth reminding ourselves that foreigners and slaves resident in Attica did not participate in public life; and by the time Athens' power crested in the latter part of the fifth century B.C., slaves and foreigners had become almost as numerous as citizens.

Moreover, the freedom and civil equality that prevailed among the Athenian citizenry depended upon the labors of distant cultivators who raised much of the grain the Athenians consumed. Like excluded peasantries the world around, these distant populations did not share directly or indirectly in the high culture generated by the city their labors helped to sustain.

Collective exploitation of distant communities is not necessarily less oppressive than similar exploitation by individual landlords or industrial entrepreneurs. Indeed it is arguable that when the exploiting collectivity is large enough, its members may be insulated from any lively fellow feeling with their victims by the sustaining force of in-group norms and standards; whereas a landlord, living in semi-isolation from his peers and close beside those whom he exploits may lack the practical means and psychological insulation required to carry exploitation to its greatest practicable extent.

Yet in ancient times, the view from within the exploiting community seemed to contradict this observation. Instead of being surrounded, as dispersed landlords must be, by peasant "inferiors," members of the privileged community were surrounded by "equals." Possibilities of open-ended and open-minded encounter within such a community were enormously enhanced. In the city's golden age, the citizens of Athens lived modestly, but all had enough to eat without working very hard. Vineyards and olive groves of the modest size ordinary Athenians possessed required some 60 to 80 days' work per annum; the rest of the time men could devote safely enough to noneconomic concerns. Indeed, the real measure of the city's wealth was the leisure its citizens enjoyed without starving.

A leisured mass of citizens several thousand strong constituted the best possible audience for anyone who had something special to say, whether about practical or theoretical questions. As a result, literary, intellectual, and artistic creativity has never been so intensely concentrated before or since, and the subsequent influence of classical Greek culture upon European (and Islamic) civilizations enhances the significance of what was then achieved.

Being first to elaborate a literary and learned tradition that has lasted uninterruptedly to the present mattered a great deal. Assumptions and biases that have been taken for granted ever since among European men of letters established themselves with comparative ease simply because there were no comparably sophisticated or clearly worked out notions about to dispute the ground. An example: no logical necessity supports the assumption that the most important human association beyond the nuclear family is the territorial state. Yet, this notion pervaded Greek and subsequent European life all the more forcefully because it was so often taken for granted. An example even more remarkable because so implausible is the bold speculation that just as human affairs could be regulated by law, recognized and agreed to in public assembly of the citizens, so also the behavior of natural objects and forces might conform to laws, if only men were clever and observant enough to discover what they were. European natural science, whose importance in recent centuries has been enormous, would be inconceivable without this assumption. Yet there is remarkably little in the behavior of earth, wind, and water, as observable to ordinary men engaged in ordinary occupations, to justify such a wild assumption. Even the movements of the heavenly bodies, when considered closely, offered stubborn resistance to being reduced to definite "laws," although persistence in what an outsider would surely have regarded as a vain pursuit did pay off after centuries of effort in the form of Ptolemy's *Almagest,* and a mechanical model of the universe that accounted for almost everything—except for such conspicuous motions as those of comets and shooting stars.

Being the first to elaborate a high culture on European soil enhanced the historical significance of ancient Greece enormously, yet I find it impossible to deny that the Athenian model of high culture had a kind of intrinsic excellence that set it apart from all other early civilizations. To be sure, the Egyptian Pharoahs of the Old Kingdom built their pyramids with a perfection unequaled later. Yet the range of Pharonic culture and its capacity for later growth was far less than that which inhered in Greek civilization. Other early classic formulations of great cultures—Confucian, Buddhist, Judaic, Islamic—that have endured to the present seem somehow narrower, perhaps because what has survived to our own times from these ancient fonts of inspiration has been encapsulated into organized religions. In the process discordancies were largely edited out. No single hand ever edited the diverse literature of ancient Greece, though the taste of generations and accidents of copy-making and survival have certainly left deep marks on our classical inheritance, and may, for instance, exaggerate the primacy of Athens by combing out texts that originated elsewhere.

Yet when all appropriate reservations have been made, there remains a special awe and reverence for what the Athenians and a few other Greeks accomplished. Who can compare with Herodotus and Thucydides among early writers of history? Or who can match Plato and Aristotle among philosophers? What literature excels Homer, Aeschylus, Sophocles, and Euripides? And classical Greek art, with its idealized naturalism and technical mastery, can surely bear comparison with any other art tradition of the earth.

In such matters there is great danger of naïveté. One praises the familiar and may be tempted to reject strange ideas and disregard alien traditions of art simply because they arouse no echoes from prior personal experience. It may therefore be a confession of my own culture-boundedness to say that the classical Greek style of civilization seems to excel all its contemporaries. Yet there is this tangible basis for such assertion: men in Macedon, Asia Minor, Scythia and central Europe, Italy, Carthage, Syria, Parthia, Egypt, and even Judea all found Greek accomplishments impressive. They proved this by borrowing aspects of Greek civilization when Alexander's conquests (334–22 B.C.) and subsequent churnings of peoples and armies throughout Mediterranean and Near Eastern lands brought the achievements of classical Greece—warlike as well as peaceable—vividly to their attention. Elements of Greek art and thought even seeped into distant India and China, modified and transformed in process of transmission all the way from one side of Asia to the other, yet recognizably continuous throughout. For more than half a millennium everybody who could do so borrowed from the Greeks. Some, like the Romans, took so much that their own traditions—save in matters of warfare, law, and government—were almost overwhelmed. As in every long drawn out cultural encounter, borrowing ran both ways. Thus the spread of mystery religions of salvation among Hellenized populations of the Mediterranean brought what had begun as a Middle Eastern religious tradition into the heart of the Greek world. But prior to about A.D. 100, religions of salvation attracted little attention among the upper classes of the Mediterranean world. They found almost everything they wanted in refined and variously watered down versions of classical Greek culture.

Throughout the fifth century, the Aegean metropolitan center of classical Greek civilization remained sharply defined. It embraced some fifty to sixty city-states located on both sides of the Aegean, where vines and olives abounded. Greek craft skills —ship building, weapons manufacture, pottery production, mining, monumental stone construction, and the like—did not differ much from professionalized levels of skill long familiar on the Syrian coast and in Asia Minor. On the other hand, the polis or city-state was distinctively Greek. In order to flourish, a polis had to command the services of a richly leisured citizenry. Otherwise the long hours spent in public business—training for the phalanx, campaigning, deliberating, administering justice, conducting diplomacy, not to mention participating in festivals and discussing matters of common concern in private gatherings of every kind—could not have been spared from the tasks of finding food enough to eat. Mass leisure was secured through the favorable terms of trade that wine and oil exporters enjoyed.

No less vital to the success of the Greek city-states were sentiments of solidarity binding all citizens together. Such feelings were built up in all young men by prolonged drill exercises, preparatory to and climaxing in the experience of battle, when each man's life depended on his neighbor's readiness to keep his place in the ranks of the phalanx. The concept of law, above and beyond any mere human will or preference, applicable to everyone and accepted knowingly by all citizens, gave intellectual form and definition to such sentiments and sustained remarkably effective cooperation among the entire body of citizens.

All these elements had to be present for classical civilization to flourish. Regions where the agricultural-commercial-industrial complex failed to take root because of climatic or other obstacles remained incapable of constructing strong and effective city-states, lacking a sufficiently leisured citizenry. Thus Thessaly and Arcadia, although inhabited by Greeks who were continuously in touch with the center of classical civilization, nonetheless remained rural, marginal, and unimportant because in these land-locked areas the requisite number of leisured citizens could not be found.

Sparta was a special case. Spartan citizens won the requisite leisure for constructing a formidable city-state by enslaving the entire population of neighboring Messenia. The Athenian pattern of trade required grain-growing landlords to exploit local peasantries living in the coast land of the Black Sea and in Sicily and southern Italy; the Spartans exported only threats to Messenia whence came the grain and other food supplies the Spartan citizens needed to be able to devote all their adult years to military training and campaigning. But the immediacy of the threat of revolt in Messenia required the Spartans to concentrate their leisure narrowly on military preparedness; the cushion—both geographical and sociological—between the Athenians and the revolutionary threat inherent in an excluded oppressed peasantry gave Athens scope for a wider range of leisure activity. Though their means of support differed in this important respect, the result was the same inasmuch as in both Sparta and Athens a sufficient body of leisured citizens with intensely shared common sentiments provided the human material from which emerged the fine flower of classical Greek civilization.

In subsequent centuries, the enormous geographical spread of aspects of Greek classical civilization involved radical transformation of the socio-economic structures that sustained its initial flowering. Leisure remained critical always; men who had to work every day just to find enough to eat were never sharers in classical civilization. But the basis of leisure shifted from the sort of collective expoitation of others which had raised Athens and Sparta to greatness. Instead, a more dispersed pattern of exploitation took over. Local landlords and tax collectors with their hangers-on gathered into small towns and cities and there set up plausible simulacra of the city-states of classical Greece—with one important difference: military power and political sovereignty were, from the age of Alexander of Macedon, snatched away from mere city-states and transferred to new sprung military monarchies, of which the last and greatest became the empire of Rome.

This vast political upheaval was matched by a dispersal of economic activity as well. The great advantages of wine and oil production meant that vineyards and olive groves tended to spread to new ground, wherever soil and climate allowed. As new sources of wine and oil came into production, the older centers sometimes lost markets, and it is likely (though data is lacking to be sure) that the relative price of oil and wine as against grain declined over the centuries from what it had been in Athens' most glorious days. The small farmers in the original Aegean heartland lost out in course of the fourth and third centuries to rival producers located mainly in Italy and Asia Minor. Italian producers, in turn, confronted disastrous market conditions in the first century A.D. when Spanish and North African oil and wines usurped western Mediterranean markets, and vines were successfully acclimated through most of Gaul all the way to the Rhine. Accordingly, from the time of the Emperor Domitian (reigned A.D. 81–96), Italy lost export markets that had been vital to the prosperity of the slave-staffed latifundia that had sprung up in the southern part of the peninsula after the Second Punic War (218–201 B.C.).

Wherever wine and oil for export commanded a substantial market, a region of relatively high prosperity was to be found—always. As such regions multiplied and dispersed toward the geographical limits of the Mediterranean world, various provinces of the Roman empire achieved a level of wealth that permitted a far-reaching reception of Graeco-Roman culture, at least among the leisured, landowning class that dominated Roman provincial society almost everywhere. But no single metropolitan center could arise and sustain itself on a commercial basis, once the original Aegean heartland had lost its initial near monopoly of such exports.

Instead, wealth and food supplies were concentrated at

political headquarters—Pella, Pergamum, Antioch, Alexandria, Rome—by a combination of predation and taxation. (The difference between the two was not always very obvious to any of the parties concerned.) The great city of Alexandria by Egypt, for example, where Hellenistic high culture had a particularly full development, lived largely on tribute paid by the Egyptian natives, from whom Ptolemy's agents extracted practically everything not required for mere survival. Industry and trade soon brought additional wealth to supplement this hard core of tax income, so that even after the Romans intervened and siphoned off for their own uses the major part of Egypt's tax yield (30 B.C.), Alexandria remained an important city and, as a matter of fact, developed a new commercial hinterland of some importance in distant India.

In the west, however, commercial-industrial development never got very far in ancient times. As the Romans extended their power throughout the Mediterranean, the city of Rome became a vast parasite. By the second century B.C., almost all of Rome's inhabitants lived directly or indirectly on plunder and taxes. After the time of Augustus (reigned 27 B.C.–A.D. 14), the Roman armies were stationed permanently along the frontiers of the empire. Among other things, this meant that a major disbursement of tax income shifted away from the city of Rome to the garrisoned provinces. This powerfully reinforced the tendency for economic prosperity to disperse toward the fringes of the Mediterranean world since the simultaneous diffusion of grape and olive cultivation moved in the same direction.

The result, therefore, was that the peculiar circumstances that had provoked and sustained the brilliant cultural innovations of the fifth century never recurred. The bearers of the Greek and Roman cultural tradition became a privileged class dispersed widely throughout the Mediterranean lands, dependent in large measure on rents and taxes for their income and surrounded by comparatively vast numbers of social inferiors with whom they shared relatively little in the way of common sentiments, ideas, or way of life. Such a milieu was not conducive to bold and restless innovation of any kind. Moreover, the easy availability of superbly attractive models of art, literature, thought, not to mention the delights of elegant eating, drinking, and sex, as worked out by the Greeks of the fifth and fourth centuries B.C., inhibited innovation still further.

There were changes of course and for a generation or two when Rome was rising to political pre-eminence, a handful of Roman writers and sculptors reacted to the collapse of customary Roman ways by using Greek patterns of thought and art to express deeply felt and profoundly serious concerns. Vergil, Cicero, Lucretius, and the artists who carved the Ara Pacis belong in this select company. They created, with others of lesser rank, a truncated version of the Athenian golden age all over again. But the Roman efflorescence did not last very long and died away without attaining richness and variety to equal the Athenian inheritance. Roman drama, for instance, remained trifling; and the historical insight and range of Livy and Tacitus fall far short of their Greek predecessors, Herodotus and Thucydides. Still, the age of Cicero and Vergil translated a goodly sample of the Greek literary and philosophic tradition into Latin, in which form it remained accessible to later generations in the west. This was significant, for the use of Latin for administrative and legal purposes spread Roman speech widely throughout the western provinces, although most of the east continued to use Greek as a lingua franca, even where older local mother tongues continued to survive, as in Egypt and Syria.

The division of the Mediterranean lands between two major linguistic provinces, one Latin, one Greek, became a lasting demarcation, reinforced and institutionalized after the third century A.D. when reforming emperors divided the empire into eastern and western halves for convenience of administration. Christian administrative lines of jurisdiction also developed in conformity to the language demarcation, so that a Latin Christendom in the western provinces emerged from the ruins of the Roman state in juxtaposition to Greek or, as it is often called, Orthodox Christendom of the eastern Mediterranean.

Because Christianity attracted the urban poor and oppressed in its initial period of growth, the church became a channel for expressing Syrian and Egyptian restlessness against and repudiation of the Greek cultural traditions which had so thoroughly seduced the upper classes since Alexander's time. When the church became powerful and attained legal rights and privileges, these sentiments found expression through divergent theological formulations, leading to schisms by which Syriac and Coptic (Egyptian) churches broke away from Greek Orthodoxy. In a similar way, Donatism in North Africa probably expressed a rising sense of cultural separatism—in this case aimed against a Latin rather than a Greek upper class—on the part of the Berber populations. These cultural and religious movements, in turn, harmonized well with the economic dispersals that had been weakening the Roman and Italian center of the empire from the time of Domitian if not before.

Graeco-Roman paganism had, indeed, become a brittle thing by the third and fourth centuries A.D. By then the lower classes of the cities had found new cultural institutions and ideals—the mystery religions in general, Christianity in particular—and felt little attraction toward any of the norms and ideals their betters had accepted—often tepidly enough—as their heritage from the, by then already ancient, Greeks. Moreover, the bearers of this attenuated tradition were no longer in any position to defend themselves against armed assault. For nearly two centuries, professionalized soldiery, stationed far away on the frontier had made local self-defense unnecessary. Then, when more formidable assault from beyond the frontiers required strenuous counter measures and far reaching military reform, as happened from the mid-third century onward, the landowning classes of the Roman provinces were unable and unwilling to do anything personally. The emperors, seeking more and more desperately for additional resources wherewith to support their greedy and unruly soldiery, resorted to confiscatory taxation. An entire class of landlords was speedily squeezed out of existence. This meant that the class which had been the main bearers of the classical tradition disappeared. New landlords came along to be sure; but they owed their position to bureaucratic and military office and often stemmed from a rude and crude soldier tradition. Repeatedly, individuals born as simple peasant boys rose to the purple through the ranks of the army. Such self-made men carried with them a multitude of similarly rough and ready colleagues and assistants, for whom the nuances of ancient Greek and Latin philosophy, art, or literature meant little or nothing.

Two important factors assured the ultimate breakup of the Roman Empire and the disruption of classical culture. First, various epidemic diseases ravaged the Mediterranean lands between the first and sixth centuries A.D., leading to widespread depopulation. Early in the Christian centuries, malaria seems to have arrived from West Africa when infectious mosquitoes succeeded in making it across the Sahara in the shelter of someone's packtrain baggage. Similarly, major new epidemic diseases seem to have penetrated the Roman world as regular and more rapid transport—caravan by land, ships by sea—began to connect the Mediterranean with diverse preexisting disease pools. As a consequence, many of what in later ages became ordinary childhood diseases—smallpox, measles, mumps, chicken pox, and the rest—probably first impinged upon Mediterranean populations in this period.

Other factors may have affected population too; but the crippling and pervasive decay of human numbers that afflicted the Roman empire after the second century A.D. was probably mainly a result of the devastating arrival of new diseases for which no previous immunities existed among the population.

Urban dwellers were, of course, particularly exposed to such infections; rural and isolated communities were best situated to survive. Individuals engaging in commerce or any other activity that required encounter with strangers and movement across country were more exposed than others. As mortality mounted, we may well believe that these facets of ancient Mediterranean society were the ones that withered fastest. Decay and retreat of market relations made effective administrative control of the state increasingly difficult. Without a ready supply of tax monies, the state had to fall back on levying taxes in kind. The compromise of dividing the empire into a number of parts, each subject to a different sovereign master, proved only a way station toward final breakup of the imperial fabric, a breakup published to the world by the Germanic invasions of the late fourth and fifth centuries.

The increased formidability of the Germans and of other barbarians beyond Roman frontiers was the other major factor contributing to the fall of Rome. Exact details are quite unknown, having never been recorded for the most part; and archaeological investigation can tell only part of the story. Still, two major developments seem well attested, and both increased the power of barbarian assault against the Roman *limes*. The first of these was the spread of a technically improved style of agriculture on the German side of the Rhine frontier; the second was the increased formidability of steppe nomads along the middle and lower Danube frontier.

Where trackless forests had prevailed in the time of Augustus, settlements of west German pioneers slowly proliferated during the first Christian centuries. As field multiplied, population grew until by the third century or so it equaled or perhaps even surpassed the density of settlement existing within Roman frontiers. The best evidence of this shift in population equilibrium is the availability of German manpower for military service in Roman armies, accompanied often by settlement of Germanic populations on the Roman side of the frontier.

It is worth asking why German farmers multiplied when agriculturalists in the Roman side of the frontier were shrinking in numbers. For many centuries German agriculture aimed only at providing subsistence to the cultivator and his family. Hence neither taxes nor trade mattered much. This, in turn, implied that disease-carrying strangers were fewer among Germans than in Gaul and Britain, where Rome's administrative and commercial framework required considerable coming and going. Second, on the Roman side of the frontier, cultivators had to part with a substantial share of their crop to tax and rent collectors. This meant less for their own support. In a year of bad harvests, famine, compounded by lack of sufficient seed for the following year's planting, presumably had more devastating demographic effects among Roman subjects than among the Germans who, as yet, had no obligation to support the burden of civilization in the form of professional administrators, soldiers, and rent receivers. Obviously, precise weighing of these factors cannot be expected, but the fact of sharply different population patterns on opposite banks of the Rhine seems certain.

The development of agriculture among the Germans was connected with the use of an improved kind of plow, capable of turning a furrow (as Mediterranean scratch plows had not done) and able to create an artificial drainage pattern on naturally flat land. Assuredly, by the fifth century A.D. when Saxon settlers crossed the North Sea to Britain, they brought with them this type of moldboard plow.[2] It made them capable of tilling the heavy clay soils of Norfolk and Suffolk where British and Roman cultivators had been unable to raise a crop. Similar techniques allowed German farmers of the lower Rhine and Weser valleys to reclaim increasing areas of what had before been waterlogged plains, covered by dense and, to the Romans, all but impenetrable forests.

The importance of this technical breakthrough was potentially enormous. Wheat and barley, the staples of Mediterranean and Middle Eastern cultivation, were naturally adapted to semiarid conditions. In the much wetter climate of northwestern Europe, Mediterranean methods of tillage had only been able to make grain flourish on specially well drained soils—chalk downs, loess, and hill tops. The potentially rich plains of northwestern Europe, lying almost flat, were mostly unusable for grain growing without the artificial drainage created by the action of the moldboard plow. Hence, the spread of such a plow, and the discovery of how effective it could be, opened broad new zones of Europe to agriculture. A new ecological niche appeared, susceptible of a vast and toilsome exploitation by the west Germans.

Multiplication of nearly self-sufficient farmsteads did not of itself create the complexities of civilization beyond the Rhine frontier. Yet population growth probably did lead to some quickening of transport by sea. The Anglo-Saxon migration to England in the fifth century A.D. proves that several thousand people were able to cross the North Sea, arriving on a shore that had been familiar to Saxon and Frisian

2. Archaeological finds provide much complicated and controversial evidence about the plows used by European cultivators in the iron age. Heavy plows that turned a furrow were known in the Ukraine and Caucasus in early times; Paul Leser, *Die Entstehung und Verbreitung des Pfluges* (Münster, 1931), even argues that the moldboard plow came to Europe from China.

pirates for some two hundred years. The swarming of the Saxons in the fifth and sixth centuries was followed in the eighth and ninth centuries by a similar swarming of Scandinavian sea rovers and emigrants. By the time the Vikings made themselves the scourge of European waterways, northern ship design and seamanship had produced an Atlantic nautical tradition roughly equivalent to, though divergent from, the far older skills of Mediterranean seamanship. Clearly, the north was catching up.

By A.D. 450 or A.D. 500, therefore, the spreading moldboard plow on the one hand and increasingly seaworthy ships on the other provided a new technical basis for the eventual flowering of high culture in northwestern Europe. But before that result could be achieved, drastic social differentiation had to occur. The free barbarian husbandman had to become a peasant paying dues and services to his social superiors. The principal impulse pushing in this direction was the need for more effective defense against raiding parties, whether coming over land on horseback, like the Huns and many another steppe nomad people, or by sea and river like the Vikings.

Before considering how Europe's cultural shape altered under these circumstances, we must backtrack briefly to consider the changes in nomad life that made the Huns and similar peoples so formidable. Two important improvements in cavalry equipment favored mounted as opposed to infantry armies during the first Christian centuries, though all details of when and where they originated remain unsure. One was the use of stirrups to give the rider a firmer seat on his horse. This simple invention benefited both bowmen and lancers. By rising out of the saddle and assuming a crouching position, a practiced rider could compensate for the vertical motion of his galloping horse. This allowed archers to shoot far more accurately from the comparative safety of a rapidly moving horse than had been possible without stirrups when riders, however skilled, bounced up and down with every stride. The advantage for lancers was even more dramatic. By leaning far forward and bracing his body against the stirrups at the moment of impact, a lancer could put the vast momentum of horse and rider behind his lance head, thereby, as Europe's medieval knights repeatedly demonstrated, achieving an all but irresistible force. Unfortunately, all details of the origin, spread, and exploitation of the military value of stirrups remain quite unclear. But in the first century A.D. this seemingly simple and obvious invention was still new among horsemen of the steppe as well as in civilized lands. In succeeding centuries, as nomads learned to exploit the possibilities of stirrups fully, the older balance of forces between infantry and cavalry was everywhere upset.

The second improvement in cavalry techniques was the introduction of a larger and stronger horse that could carry armor and an armored man without difficulty. This seems to have developed among Iranians in the first century B.C., perhaps when they found out that by cultivating alfalfa they could produce suitable and sufficient winter fodder to keep even large and hungry horses in shape. Such beasts remained exceedingly expensive to maintain, and on the open steppe the small tough pony, capable of scraping a living even in winter from beneath the snow, remained the normal nomad mount. The big horse suited the shock tactics of the lance better than any smaller mount could do, and its importance was confined to places where these tactics prevailed over archery. On the steppe itself, the bow remained supreme as it had been even before stirrups so greatly increased the accuracy of archery from horseback.

Technical changes of this magnitude accompanied and presumably provoked or at least permitted large scale migrations and conquests to sweep the European steppe. Before the Huns appeared on the scene from somewhere further east, the penetration of Germanic speaking Goths from the north, beginning in the second century A.D., created considerable upheaval. Warfare and plundering associated with this change of sovereignty may have damaged agricultural communities on and adjacent to the steppe lands before the Huns ruthlessly carried harassment and extermination to a new height. The Hunnic empire lasted a mere eighty-five years to be sure; but the Huns were succeeded by a seemingly unending flow of Avars, Bulgars, Khazars, Pechenegs, Magyars. Each nomad wave pushed back the limits of agricultural settlement further, so that during the six hundred and more years, from 370, when the Huns crossed the Don, until 896, when the Magyars crossed the Carpathians, the natural grasslands of eastern Europe were reclaimed for nomadry. Even in naturally forested lands, many places where cultivation once had flourished were abandoned and went back to woods.

If we try for a synoptic view, therefore, we may say that the regions north of the Roman frontiers entered upon a sort of enormous seesaw during the first millennium of the Christian era. A substantial development of agriculture took place in the west, and barriers to cultivation that had prevented dense occupation of the plains of northwestern Europe were permanently broken through. In the east an opposite trend prevailed, as the increased formidability of horse nomad peoples tended to drive agriculture from the grasslands, where it had never made more than modest lodgement and created a zone adjacent to the regions of open grass where agricultural settlement in forested lands remained thin and precarious.

Within the Mediterranean zone, too, a sort of east-west seesaw occurred during the same centuries, but in an opposite sense, for there it was the east that reasserted itself, while the wealth and power of western Mediterranean regions diminished. Italy, Gaul, and Spain failed to keep pace with the Aegean and Asian Minor coastlands. High skills disappeared from these western Mediterranean lands because organizing (and dominating) centers could not sustain themselves effectively over more than limited local areas. After the prolonged military upheavals of the third century (A.D. 235–85), the city of Rome ceased to be a major seat of government. Italy had long since ceased to receive significant tribute income from the provinces, so that the concentration of wealth which had supported the brief efflorescence of Roman culture dissipated long before the imperial structure decayed. The emperors of the third and fourth centuries, having abandoned Rome, set up headquarters nearer threatened frontiers where local food resources were available to feed a substantial body of troops or where lines of communication made it relatively easy to concentrate supplies from a distance.

By far the best such location was on the Bosporus, where Constantine the Great renamed the ancient Greek city of Byzantium after himself when he made it his capital in A.D. 330. The Aegean and Black sea waterways converged at Constantinople, making it possible to move goods and armies to and fro, even across long distances, with comparative ease. This in turn meant that a reasonably effective central power could be maintained from such a headquarters. Taxes (whether in goods or money) could be concentrated in the capital and used to support an army and navy strong enough to overawe most rivals and, as it turned out, capable in a pinch of defending the walls of Constantinople against all comers for nearly a thousand years. When one part of the city's hinterland had been ravaged and depopulated, whether by nomad raiders or through some other form of disaster, other sections of the accessible coastlands could be counted on to escape damage and be available, therefore, to feed the capital and sustain the imperial administrative and military machinery until such time as local recovery allowed the devastated regions once again to contribute their share to the support of the central power. Similarly, even if command of the Aegean might be lost for a while, as it was in the ninth century to Moslem seafarers from the south, command of the Black Sea and its connecting waters offered the empire a viable, if reduced, means for concentrating resources. Conversely, loss of control of the Black Sea to Varangian raiding parties could be countered by means of resources concentrated from Aegean coastlands.

The unique geopolitical advantages of such a capital (reinforced by formidable walls and a good natural harbor) do much to account for the survival of the Roman empire in the east long after it had vanished from the west, where no remotely comparable location for imperial headquarters existed. Moreover, the survival of an effective imperial administration generated commerce and industry, since the goods and tax monies brought together in the capital never of themselves sufficed to equip the soldiers, ships, and courtiers with exactly the assortment of things needed and desired. Imperial and private workshops were required to turn raw materials into suitable end products. Similarly, tax monies filtered back to the provinces whence they had come whenever officials and soldiers used cash to buy commodities produced in the provinces. Industry and commerce in turn sustained town life and the relatively complex social stratification that urbanism implied.

On this basis, a relatively high state of civilization could be and was maintained in Constantinople and a few other major cities of the eastern Mediterranean. The sociopolitical regime was more like that of ancient Near Eastern empires—Persian, Assyrian, Babylonian—than like that of classical Greece, and there is perhaps more than symbolic significance in the fact that from the time of Diocletian (reigned 285–305) the Roman emperors used insignia of office borrowed from Persian kings. Similarly, the dominant place held by the Christian church after Constantine's time in all matters intellectual and for the patronage of art gave the high culture of the East Roman or Byzantine empire a strong "oriental" flavor.

Yet it would be unfair to emphasize the derivative character of Byzantine civilization unduly. The originality and power of Byzantine high culture survives for us mainly through art. In thought and letters there is less to admire. Learned Byzantines decried innovation, for innovation implied some inadequacy in the inherited traditions of the past, and the revealed truths of Christianity could not, by definition, lack anything essential. Such stoutly conservative views gained urgency as a result of the bitter doctrinal controversies of the fourth to sixth centuries that subsided only when dissident Syriac and Coptic Christians, not to mention Donatists of North Africa and Arians in Spain, passed under Moslem political control between 636 and 711. Thereafter a rigid definition of Orthodoxy defied alteration, even when the emperors themselves (perhaps deferring to Moslem reproaches of idolatry) attempted to banish sacred images from the churches.

Yet in spite of the professed conservatism of Byzantine thought and the pervasive ritualism of Byzantine practice, it seems just to concur with the long standing historiographical tradition that recognizes both Byzantines and Moslems as bearers of new civilizations. Graeco-Roman and ancient Near Eastern (mainly Hebraic) elements intermingled to shape both the Byzantine and Moslem civilizations, and despite the obvious and deeply felt doctrinal differences that divided them, there was much they shared. Convention, however, treats Moslem history and civilization as not part of the history of Europe, and for the purpose of this essay it seems best to conform to this view and acquiesce in breaking up the cultural unity of the Mediterranean that had prevailed in Roman times.

Leaving Islam to one side, therefore, it remains to consider the state of Europe about A.D. 900 when the two vast seesaw movements, mentioned above, had had time to work themselves out.

First and most important: the Byzantine center far exceeded anything existing elsewhere in Europe at the time. Byzantine art, ceremonial, artisan skills, administration, diplomacy, and literary sophistication all surpassed their analogues in any other part of Europe, and were rivaled or exceeded only in the great centers of Islam—Baghdad, Damascus, Cairo. Yet the centrality of dogmatic religion in Byzantine civilization meant that those who rejected the Orthodox definition of Christian truth were also also prone to reject Byzantine culture as a whole. Such attitudes, reciprocated from each side, insulated Moslems from Christians far more effectively than their propinquity and shared cultural ancestry would suggest; and within Christendom a similar though less pronounced barrier divided Greek from Latin Christians.

Memories of the Roman past, when the west had dominated the east, remained alive, especially in Latin ecclesiastical circles. Among laymen, barbarian pride in personal prowess made it possible for crude warriors to sneer at the effete, urban, and (at least sometimes) urbane Greeks who governed the Byzantine state and society. Among Slavs of the Balkans and Russia, however, competing models of civilization were too distant to matter, with the exception of Islam, which soon became identified with the nomad raiders of the steppe—the Slavs' perpetual and dangerous enemy. Hence the major field of cultural expansion for Byzantines lay northward into Russia and inland from the Aegean coasts toward the Balkan interior. In A.D. 900, penetration of Byzantine culture along the Russian rivers and into the Balkans was still in its initial stages; but the pattern of acculturation was relatively straightforward, with Constantinople (and Mt. Athos monasteries) serving as a model, while lesser courts and capitals and their associated monasteries did all they could to imitate the imperial example.

In western Europe, the situation was less clearly defined. The Popes of Rome aspired to exert an imperial sway in matters ecclesiastical and did indeed organize successful missionary efforts in England and much of Germany. There were, however, rival aspirants to imperial rank in western Europe, namely the Frankish kings. Their power centered on the middle and lower Rhine, but extended widely into Gaul, Germany, and northern Italy. The greatest of these kings, Charlemagne (reigned 768–814), took the imperial title on Christmas Day, 800 and later was able to persuade officials in Byzantium to recognize his legitimacy as a successor of the Roman emperors of the west.

But the Carolingian empire lacked a capital capable of playing the role Constantinople played in the Byzantine state. Indeed, Charlemagne, like his predecessors, had to move around continually in order to feed himself and his court—it being easier to move a few hundred persons to and fro than it was to concentrate sufficient food and other supplies at one place to maintain the court throughout the year. A military campaign practically every summer went along with this itinerant style of life; and the numerous, hardy footsoldiers who regularly went to war under Charlemagne's command gave the Franks numerical advantage over most foes. When the striking power of a few heavy cavalrymen, specially equipped with armor and lances, was added to the Frankish host (an innovation attributable to Charlemagne's grandfather, Charles Martel), a formidable force capable of routing almost any foe within reach came into existence. The enormous size of Charlemagne's empire was the result.

Yet against enemies who could move rapidly, whether by land like the Magyars on their light steppe ponies, or by sea like the Vikings who began to harass Carolingian coasts during Charlemagne's own lifetime, the Frankish host was ineffective. It took too long to assemble, and it moved no faster than a man could walk. Mobile raiders could easily outstrip such a force, plundering at will. The vast bulk of the Carolingian state, therefore, proved easily vulnerable and swiftly disintegrated in all but name in the century after Charlemagne's death.

Papal aspirations were vulnerable too. As long as Carolingian and other German kings wished to maintain good relations with the Pope, the lay power supported ecclesiastical centralization. In return, German rulers could expect the sanction of religion for their rather fumbling efforts at extending royal jurisdiction beyond their functions as war leader, which they had inherited from the barbarian and pagan past. But in proportion as such rulers lost power, being unable even to fulfill their traditional roles of war captain successfully against Magyar and Viking attack (supplemented in the Mediterranean by Moslem pirates), the church, too, lost even the appearance of order and discipline. The Pope, like many another bishop, became a pawn in the hands of local armed cliques, seeking whatever advantage was to be gained from putting one of its partisans in episcopal office.

Neither the Germanic center in the Rhinelands nor the ecclesiastical center in Italy therefore succeeded before A.D. 900 in organizing itself into a genuinely effective dominating center for western Europe as a whole. Communications were too slow, local self-sufficiency too prevalent to permit any other result.

On the extreme periphery of the continent, first Ireland and then Scandinavia began to create distinctive local styles of civilization which, under other circumstances, might have grown into effective rivals to Rome and the Rhinelands. But the Irish monasteries were destroyed by Viking raids, and the vigor and attractiveness of Celtic Christian culture (demonstrated by some remarkable missionary careers in Great Britain and on the continent) soon faded away thereafter. As for the Vikings themselves, their roving brought them into touch with all of Europe's varying styles of high culture, whether Byzantine or Roman, English, Irish or Frankish. Their indigenous paganism was unable to resist Christianity for very long, particularly when aspiring kings, needing religious sanction for their efforts at state building, found it convenient to make acceptance of Christian baptism equivalent to a loyalty oath and equated paganism with rebellion.

Finally, a word about Spain. Conquered by Moslems from North Africa in the years after 711, the Iberian peninsula became politically separated from the rest of Islam after 755 when a scion of the dispossessed Ummayad dynasty made good his claim to sovereignty. The dynasty lasted until 1031, and during much of that time maintained a brilliant court at Cordova. Ummayad sovereigns strove, as a matter of policy, to make their court a worthy rival to the Abbasid capital of Baghdad. They often came close; but the Christians of Spain, and a fortiori Christians beyond the Pyrenees, paid little attention. Spain's cultural hinterland lay across the Straits of Gibraltar, in Morocco and adjacent parts of Africa. As such, this far western Moslem presence in Europe, though it endured more than 600 years in all, perhaps deserves to be omitted from the ambit of European history, as is conventionally done in (largely unwitting) deference to later Spanish religious and national prejudices against the Moors.

In sum: this chapter has tried to sketch a great pulsation in European history. The story begins about 900 B.C. when the disorders and dispersals incident to the Dorian invasions of Greece began to subside and classical civilization started to take shape. It ends with a similar movement of peoples accompanying the collapse of Roman administration in the western provinces of the Empire. In between, classical Greek civilization came sharply and marvelously into focus in the Aegean Basin between, say, 490 and 322 B.C. Thereafter the Greek model carried everything before it. With the political unification of all Mediterranean lands by the Romans, a relatively coherent pattern emerged whereby the Graeco-Roman civilized style of life spread thinly throughout the Mediterranean lands, while beyond the Rhine and Danube frontiers barbarian freedom and simplicity shaded off into the isolated autonomy of hunters and gatherers of the far north. Economic decentralization within the Mediterranean zone soon was followed by political breakup of the Roman state. This inaugurated a more complicated pattern, whereby a revived and somewhat displaced Greek metropolitan center arose around Constantinople in the east, whereas elsewhere in Europe a number of competing—or at least divergent—styles of life came into existence without organizing themselves clearly around any single metropolitan center, save insofar as Byzantium played that role for all of Christian Europe. After A.D. 900, however, a more distinct and powerful cultural ensemble emerged in the northwest; and with that development Europe attained what we may perhaps appropriately call its medieval configuration. The next chapter will explore its major lineaments.

IV
EUROPE, 900–1500

In A.D. 900 most of Europe was thinly settled. Communications were erratic, piracy rife. Most men lived and died close to home; a few went raiding, sometimes across great distances. Since raiding never turned up exactly the sorts of goods a war band needed to keep going, even the fiercest raiders had to supplement their rapine with more peaceable commerce by seeking out spots where weapons, sails and oars, food, horses, falcons, jewelry, and other necessary or desirable commodities could be had from suppliers who themselves hovered perpetually between haggling over a price and resorting to armed force as a way of making a living. In Byzantium and a few other cities of the Aegean-Black Sea area, cities existed with their artisans, merchants, soldiers, tax collectors, rentiers, and other specialists; the same was true of Moslem Spain. Elsewhere in Europe, itinerant royal courts, monasteries, or a bishop's seat served the functions cities performed in the two more civilized parts of the continents. They often acted as cities only during a few days of the year when a fair brought local people and a sprinkling of strangers together to do business for a limited period of time.

By 1500, a great change had taken place. Cities had spread

widely through the continent; ships traveled regularly to and fro between the northern and Mediterranean seas; peaceable commerce had far outstripped piracy and raiding as a way of making a living. Population had grown. Except for the tundra of the far north where Lapps roamed freely with their reindeer, states, administered from a fixed center, had established their power throughout the continent. Civilization, in a word, had spread northward from the Spanish and Byzantine bridgeheads of 900, engulfing almost the whole of Europe. Geographical and climatic boundaries that had checked the diffusion of classical civilization had been triumphantly broken through. The Rhine, which had been the utmost boundary of civilized patterns of life in Roman times, became axial for the high culture of the northwest; and in the east the Russian rivers had likewise begun to support state building, trade, and other traits of civilization despite persistent agricultural poverty. Yet until a century or more after 1500, the primacy of the Mediterranean lands remained, in most respects, unshaken, despite increasingly vigorous currents of cultural creativity manifested in the north.

By A.D. 900, the Viking raids, which had been so destructive to Irish, English, and Frankish societies, were changing character. Instead of returning to the chill twilight of the Scandinavian north, Viking crews began to spend the winter in softer, more southerly climes, at river mouths or some other convenient location. Resulting liaisons with local women soon called into existence a new generation of formidable warriors who more often than not spoke the language of their mothers —Flemish, French, Russian, English, or Gaelic, as the case might be. Simultaneously, the increased wealth and sophistication that successful raids brought to the northlands stimulated efforts at state building in Denmark, Norway, and Sweden.

As had happened in preceding centuries among the Germans, the aspiring monarchs of the Scandinavian north found a very useful ally in the Christian church. The pomp and mystery of Christian services plus the hope of salvation attracted barbarians of all ranks to Christianity. But what made the religion especially dear to would-be rulers was Christian teaching about kingship, which accorded to them the rights and majesty ancient Near Eastern monarchs and Roman Emperors had actually enjoyed. Such an ideal of kingship constituted an irresistibly attractive agendum for barbarian war captains seeking to make their power secure, hereditary, and effective in peace as well as on the battlefield.

For a while it looked as though the Scandinavian thrust toward monarchy and centralization might succeed in building two impressive and extensive imperial structures: a Danish empire of the northern seas and a Varangian empire of the Russian rivers, headquartered at Kiev. But the Danish sea empire collapsed after the death of Canute the Great in 1025; and the empire of the Russian rivers disintegrated after the death of Yaroslav the Wise in 1054. Before their break up both these state structures attained impressive size. Canute controlled the shores of the North Sea, including parts of Denmark, England, Scotland, and Norway; Yaroslav's empire extended from Novgorod in the north to the lower Volga and lower Danube in the south.

Needless to say, both states depended on movement of men and goods by ship and were held together by very elementary administrative structures. To command such an empire, the monarch had to be, like Agamemnon of old, a hero in his own person. Only a king who embodied the warrior ideal of reckless courage, boundless generosity, unwavering loyalty could attract and hold a corps of fellow heroes, whose valor and faithfulness to him was the critical factor making the central power as formidable as it was. But the heroic style of life was incompatible with niggling attention to routine administration; still less was it consonant with money grubbing efforts to collect taxes and concentrate resources in a central treasury. As a result, when a great captain such as Canute or Yaroslav died, his state vanished with him overnight, leaving only quarreling fragments behind.

External forces also had something to do with the failure of these imperial states. In the west, vastly improved local self-defense—the feudal system—made raiding unprofitable and thereby deprived sea kings of easy access to booty income that was important, perhaps essential, for maintaining their following of fellow heroes. In the east, new hordes of steppe nomads, fresh from central Asia intruded upon the river-based empire of the Varangians by taking control of its southern portion. Yaroslav's heirs were unable to repel them successfully, since the mobility and local self-sufficiency of mounted archers was on the whole superior to that of swordsmen who had to move mainly by river and who lacked the skill with the bow that made the warriors of the steppe so formidable in battle.

The combination of internal fragility and external pressures therefore wiped away most traces of both these northern empires rather quickly. Their lasting mark upon the face of Europe was a result of the royal policy of alliance with and patronage of the Christian church. Newly founded monasteries and cathedrals acted as foyers for the propagation of literacy and of the intellectual and artistic traditions of Christianity as defined and perfected in such great centers a Byzantium, Mount Athos, Canterbury, and Rome. Landmark dates were the establishment of Christianity as the official faith in Kiev (989) and Norway (by 1000).

The intrinsic attractions of Christian faith and culture, consistently supported by princely policy made such conversions permanent. The establishment of Christianity initially made bishops and abbots into allies and servants of royal power; yet Church-administered law and ecclesiastical property rights also had the effect of limiting secular authority. This produced a deep seated duality in European loyalties and ideals. The fact that later on many prelates identified themselves with the landed nobility reinforced this dualism, multiplying local support for ecclesiastical autonomy. In return, the literacy and learning associated with the church conferred upon nobles almost the same advantages churchmen had initially brought to kingship. For documentary attestation of property rights became in time more important for protecting a noble landowner against greedy agents of the central government than mere brute force.

During the same period of time, parallel changes cushioned central and western Europe from the risk of nomad raiding from the steppes. State building first among Bulgars, then among Magyars led, as was happening simultaneously in Scandinavia, to the introduction of Christianity under royal auspices. The effect was to bring the lower and middle Danube plains within the circle of Christian culture by 1001, when St. Stephen of Hungary's coronation was solemnized with a crown provided for the purpose by the Pope of Rome. External checks to the sort of raids that had been successful earlier contributed to the conversion and internal consolidation of both Bulgar and Magyar states. Collision with a revivified Byzantine military machine convinced the Bulgar khans that they should apprentice themselves as vigorously as possible to Byzantine civilization. In 1018, the apprenticeship terminated with the conquest of the Bulgarian empire and its full incorporation into the Byzantine domain. For the Magyars, the defeat they suffered at the hands of German forces in 955 (Battle of Lechfeld) had an analogous effect, convincing the Magyar court that Christian civilization in the German mold offered a model to be imitated insofar as possible.

North of the Danube and eastward across the Ukrainian steppes, however, no comparable political-cultural transformation occurred. The arrival of new Turkish tribes from the east —Pechenegs and Cumans—reinforced pagan, nomadic traditions just at the time when the Magyars and Scandinavians decided to apprentice themselves to Christian patterns of culture. When the newcomers felt the need of civilization, they turned toward Islam rather than toward Christianity. Affinities derived from central Asia where Turks and Moslems had long been in contact, contributed to this pattern of preference; the activity of Moslem merchant-missionaries in the steppelands, and affinities with nomadic life deriving from the Arabian background of Islam itself also played a part.

In effect, therefore, what we see happening by 1000 or thereabouts is that three distinct southern centers of high culture began to stake out definite provinces in the north: Rome and the Papacy exerted vague but real influence among the Latin and Germanic peoples, flanked by Celts on one fringe and Magyars on the other, defining amongst them the realm of Latin Christendom. Eastward, Byzantium was strengthening its influence upon the Slavs and Rumanians of the Balkan interior as well as north of the Black Sea in Russia. Simultaneously, Baghdad developed its own field of force among the Turkish-speaking nomads of the Ukrainian steppes.

The remaining center of high culture within Europe, Moslem Spain, continued to influence a vast hinterland extending across North and seeping into West Africa; but until the thirteenth century, so far as I know, Moslem Spanish civilization exerted almost no overt attraction upon the rude frontier fighters of the Christian north. Like Turkish nomads of the Ukraine, the Spanish frontiersmen armored themselves against the seductions of civilization in the form most accessible to them by a nominal, but belligerent, adherence to a rival form of religion. By espousing Christianity or Islam, as the case might be, border raids became Holy Wars, taking booty was sanctified, and a predatory way of life acquired the support of organized religion. Fanatic barbarism therefore survived across both the Spanish and the Ukrainian frontiers longer than elsewhere in Europe.[1]

In the three centuries that followed this definition of Europe's cultural patterns, 1000–1300, two great changes occurred. In the Mediterranean area, both the Byzantine and the Spanish Moslem centers of civilization underwent drastic disruption. In the middle of the Mediterranean, however, Italy gathered to itself enhanced wealth, power, and cultural influence, becoming, indeed, the metropolitan center par excellence of all Europe.

This shift toward the center in the Mediterranean coincided with a contrasting trans-Alpine pattern. In the northwest, a newly defined style of civilization and society achieved remarkable success and drew the allegiance of a very considerable part of all Europe, outstripping Italy itself in some important respects, especially in the thirteenth century. In the same century, the basin of the middle and lower Volga became the seat of a Mongol-Turkish style of life that dominated almost all of Russia in matters military and economic, although Christianity continued to set the Russian population apart from their new (presently Moslem) masters.

Of these great fluctuations, the most familiar and that which mattered most for the long term future, was the rise of a new civilized style of life in northwestern Europe. The technical basis for the remarkable upthrust which occurred between 1000 and 1300 in the region between the Loire and

1. The frontier between the Scottish highlands and lowlands shows, however, that religious sanctification was not necessary for survival of a barbarous style of life into the eighteenth century.

the Rhine (with the southeastern part of Great Britain as a not unimportant outlier across the Channel) had been laid in the previous era. These were the spread of moldboard agriculture, the development of shipping, and the invention of the cavalry tactics that made Frankish knights so terrible in battle. Improvements in detail continued after 1000; but the real difference was the vast increase of the scale upon which these new technologies were applied. The disasters and upheavals of the Viking age certainly erased barriers to use of the moldboard plow which had checked its spread for centuries. Local survivors of a Viking raid had no incentive to maintain old obstructive field boundaries and property lines, and every inducement to pool resources for tillage, as the moldboard plow required, since the four, six, eight, or even twelve oxen needed to drive it through the soil were more than any ordinary cultivator could supply by himself.[2]

Similarly, the essentials of knightly cavalry tactics had been developed at the court of Charles Martel by 732, but for a long time the heavy expense of equipping and maintaining an armored horse and man made such warriors rare. When, however, local defense against Viking and/or Magyar attack

2. Scratch plow cultivation required cross plowing, that is, dragging the share in one direction through the field and then across more or less at right angles to break up the soil more efficiently. This was best done in square, or nearly square fields. The moldboard plow, on the contrary, turned a furrow which could not be disturbed without spoiling the drainage pattern furrows created in the field. But the plow and its team was awkward to turn. Hence long (220 yards by convention) and narrow field shapes alone suited the moldboard plow. Only by abandoning old field boundaries and property lines could an established agricultural community shift from one to the other technique of cultivation; and in normal times resistance to such a step was obviously enormous. By breaking normal resistance to such innovation, Viking ravagers greatly accelerated the spread of moldboard cultivation which, once established as the norm, made almost all the forest land of northwest Europe into potentially fertile fields.

became critical, German freeman as much as ex-Roman *coloni* agreed that even heavy payment for the support of a knight perpetually in residence and on call was better than periodic exposure to devastating raids. As this became clear to all concerned, the feudal system burgeoned. Counts and other administrators enfeoffed knights who promised military service in return for rights to collect income from one or more villages.

From the peasant point of view, the enhanced efficiency of moldboard cultivation and the possibility of putting new forest lands into cultivation as rapidly as available man and ox power permitted, made support of a knight comparatively easy to bear. As a result, knights soon became numerous enough to form a formidable defense against raiders. Even a dozen knights, assembled on short notice from a radius of three or four miles, could take on a raiding ships' crew and expect victory, since in hand to hand combat the mounted and armored man had an enormous advantage over footsoldiers, however brave and numerous.

The knight's superiority over Magyar horse archers was far less, since it was difficult for knights on their heavy horses to close with the Magyars' ponies. Consequently, the spread of knighthood and of the social structure required to support a numerous class of knights was slower in central and eastern Germany than it was in the regions exposed to Viking harassment. Older forms of social organization—the stem or tribal duchies—persisted longer, and the importance of the knightly class, with its heroic and chivalric ideals, was never as great as in the northwesternmost parts of Europe.

Politically, the consequences were what one would expect. Effective defense on a local basis implied decay and all but disappearance of larger political units on the North Sea and Channel coastlands. In the interior of Germany, however, tribal and ecclesiastical authority mattered more, locally supported knights amounted to less, and from 962 Otto the Great's revived Imperial title carried with it the claim to primacy in all of Latin Christendom, like Charlemagne if not exactly like Caesar.

As raiding became costly and dangerous in more and more localities, the alternative of peaceful trade forcefully recommended itself to the ships' crews that continued to sail the northern seas in search of anything they could find to supplement the short rations available at home—whether home was in Scandinavia or in some port of the southlands. The knightly class, with a claim to rents and services from peasant cultivators attached to each fief by law and custom, was in an excellent position to accumulate surplus food and other commodities; and as trade developed, even the most heroic warriors soon learned that such surpluses could be exchanged for fine clothes and luxuries as well as for items they needed for success in battle—armor, weapons, war horses.

Presently, traders settled in places where communications lines met, built walls for their protection, and organized a town government to make sure that all who benefited from such local improvements helped to pay for them. Artisans, in turn, quickly clustered within town walls. Other kinds of experts soon appeared: teachers, preachers, doctors, lawyers, and the like. The panoply of civilization thus rapidly developed in northwestern Europe, sustained and fed by rapidly expanding agriculture, biting into the vast virgin forests that initially surrounded the cleared fields of each village. The expansion of tillage was sustained by rapid population growth, which spilled over from the countryside into the numerous towns that soon dotted the landscape.

Boom times continued until about 1270. By then nearly all suitable land had been brought under cultivation. Any further clearance cut into woodlands which were needed to supply fuel and for other uses. In other words, after some three centuries of extraordinary expansion, in the regions where the new balance between man and nature based upon moldboard agriculture had met with its first massive success, natural limits had been reached. After about 1270, the disappearance of adequate woodlands—something that would have seemed inconceivable in 900 when forests were everywhere—began to put a powerful brake on any further expansion of the economy, and in some places made maintenance of what had already been achieved impossible.

This check was postponed and its impact reduced by emigration. Pioneer settlers confronted a broad belt of woodlands to the east. Clearance of land beyond the Elbe went steadily forward until the fifteenth century, with help from emigrants from the densely occupied core area on either side of the lower Rhine. But as cultivators moved eastward, conditions of soil and climate became less propitious. Even when they used exactly the same tools and methods as those familiar on the fertile lands of the northwest, they got poorer harvests and could therefore support fewer professionalized fighting men, clergymen, townsmen, and other sorts of social superior.

In Croatia, Bohemia, and part of Poland, Slavs took up the moldboard plow; elsewhere the frontier of this sort of cultivation pretty well coincided with the limits of German settlement. Further east, farmers did not take to the heavy plow, partly because it required changes in habits of work, but mainly because it cost more to build and operate and did not increase yields sufficiently under eastern European conditions to make the extra costs worthwhile. Instead, in the generally dryer conditions of eastern Europe, a shifting style of cultivation, using a light scratch plow like that long familiar in Mediterranean lands sufficed. The boundary line between the long acre fields required by the moldboard plow and the squarish, irregularly shaped fields appropriate to scratch plow cultivation still runs through Europe and provides a tangible indication of exactly where pioneer settlers from the northwest reached the effective limit of their expansion.[3]

Simultaneously, a different kind of emigration spread the fame of western or "Franklish" knighthood far and wide across Europe and into the heartlands of Islam itself. In the eleventh century, having everywhere turned back barbarian invaders, knights took the offensive across every frontier of Latin Christendom. Younger sons and other restless fighting men of western Europe rallied behind enterprising adventurers who led bands of a few hundred or thousand knights in a remarkable series of conquests. Normans, that is, the Frenchified heirs of northmen settled around the mouth of the Seine, played a particularly distinguished role in this expansion, beginning with Duke William's conquest of England in 1066 and Robert Guiscard's no less remarkable conquest of southern Italy and his brother's conquest of Sicily between 1057 and 1091. Normans and Flemings played a leading part in the even more spectacular First Crusade (1097–99) which penetrated all the way to Jerusalem and established a string of Christian states along the Syrian and Palestinian coasts.

3. This eastward movement revived from time to time in later centuries, especially in the eighteenth, when the Austrian and Russian bureaucracies systematically recruited German settlers from Swabia and elsewhere in the west to occupy land in the Danube, Dnieper, and Volga valleys which had been newly won from nomad Turkish control. There settlers brought their plows and field shapes with them, creating islands of long acre cultivation in the sea of scratch plow shifting agriculture that continued to dominate east European landscapes until the twentieth century. Successful eighteenth century colonization was, however, limited to unusually fertile soils, and usually required (or at least enjoyed) partial exemption from rent and/or tax payments assessed on other communities. By and large, it therefore appears that by 1500 or earlier, moldboard agriculture had in fact reached the geographic limits within which it was economically more efficient than scratch plow cultivation. Eventually, tractors pulling plows designed for high speed operation altered this balance, but only in the twentieth century.

In the north, German knights extended their domain across the Elbe and then, in the thirteenth century, having been checked in their eastward expansion by a consolidated Polish state, leap-frogged to Prussia and then along the Baltic coast as far as the Gulf of Finland. The second phase of this expansion was carried through by the Teutonic Order, a crusading society of knights. German settlers occupied Prussia; elsewhere the knights subjected local peoples—Lithuanians, Latvians, Esthonians—but populated the towns for the most part with German immigrants. (In fact, German and Germanized [often Jewish] townsmen outstripped German rural settlement everywhere along this eastward frontier, penetrating Poland, Bohemia, and Hungary where Slavic and Magyar peasants worked the fields.)

This enormous economic and military success provided a basis for an equally remarkable elaboration of high culture. Romanesque gave way to Gothic art with an energy and driving self-confidence that is reminiscent of the pride and skill with which classical Greek art burst forth to celebrate the perfection of the polis. But it was Latin Christian civilization, bodied forth in a series of great cathedrals that demanded celebration in the thirteenth century; and townmen's pride, reinforced by the piety of poor peasants and of lordly rent receivers of high and low degree, found full throated expression in lofty naves and the tracery of Gothic windows and spires. The power and exuberance of Gothic art paralleled the development of rational theology at the University of Paris, itself a new institution devoted as much to the definition and discovery of truth as to its propagation.

The buoyancy and sublime self-confidence which characterized the culture of northwestern Europe in the thirteenth century was sustained by the massive economic and military successes which continued to reward Frankish efforts to cope with nature and with men of alien culture. In such circumstances,

Latin Christians could afford to be curious and were willing and ready to interrogate ancients and moderns who had anything interesting to say. The reception of Aristotelian philosophy and of much of Greek science in Paris in the thirteenth century is, of course, the great example of this openness to novelty and of confidence in human reason as a guide to nature and the universe. The reception of Roman law in Bologna and at other centers (mainly in Italy) was a second and equally important demonstration of Latin Christendom's confidence in reason as a guide to ordering society. In addition, Arabic poetry, Celtic myths, pagan antiquity, whether Roman or German—all provided stimuli for the flowering of literature.

Institutional inventiveness was no less striking. Guilds, parliaments, and innumerable other corporations for the conduct of economic and religious as well as political affairs proliferated freely. These corporations allowed individuals to cooperate more and more effectively across time and space; and the aptitude Latin Christians exhibited for this form of endeavor magnified their power and multiplied efficiency as compared to anything attainable in communities where men were less able or willing to trust one another. The all but universal training peasants had in cooperation through joint tillage of open fields perhaps underlay and reinforced such aptitudes; at any rate the dense multiplication of corporative associations capable of ordering and compartmentalizing human activity seems clearly to coincide geographically with the distribution of moldboard tillage in Europe. Beyond those limits, distrust of persons beyond the circle of blood relationship tended to interfere with the smooth functioning of such corporations, and masculine personal self-assertion often proved incompatible with voluntary acceptance of subordinate roles in corporate undertakings.

Consolidation of comparatively large kingdoms in both

France and England was another illustration of the vigor of institutional inventiveness that characterized the heartlands of this northwestern style of civilization. But territorial sovereignties, however delineated on the ground, never achieved the unambiguous primacy among human associations that they had been accorded among the ancient Greeks. Overlapping jurisdictions were the rule; in particular, the claims of the Church to universal sway—if not over bodies at least over souls—tempered and often conflicted with secular rulers' power. Local and customary ties between knight and peasant, landlord and tenants, also countervailed centralizing, bureaucratic tendencies; and in the Germanies and part of Italy, the overarching claims of an emperor met effective opposition from lesser territorial princes on the one hand, and from rival claims to universal authority issuing from the Popes in Rome on the other.

Assuredly, the brilliant achievements of Latin Christendom in the tenth to thirteenth centuries deserve the attention historians have lavished upon this age. Modern western civilization, which bestrode the entire world like a colossus in the eighteenth and nineteenth centuries, grew from these roots. The medieval history of the Seine, Rhine, and Thames basins have, therefore, a peculiar importance for those who hope to understand our own times. Nor is modern reverence for the achievements of the thirteenth century in northwestern Europe merely romantic retrospection. Men in the age itself and in the century that followed recognized the attractiveness of what had been so triumphantly generated on the soil of northern France and adjacent regions. The reception of Gothic art and Parisian scholasticism in Italy itself, not to mention the diffusion of these styles of art and of thought throughout central and eastern Europe as far as the limits of moldboard cultivation, proves it. The *reconquista* of Spain by knights armed and trained *a la Franca* and the subjugation of the Celtic fringes of the British Isles by Norman conquerors and churchmen between the twelfth and fourteenth centuries also attested the enduring power of the Frankish style of life. The capture of Constantinople in 1204 by knights of the Fourth Crusade and the establishment of a number of Frankish principalities in the Levant thereafter were yet other demonstrations of the power Europe's far west had achieved. Frankish styles of warfare and courtly culture even made modest inroads among the Greeks and other Balkan Christians in the thirteenth to fourteenth centuries. Russia itself turned back the knightly assault only by accepting Mongol rule.

Yet it is a defect of perspective to treat this brilliant Frankish civilization as the only important cultural model in medieval Europe. At the beginning of the period with which we are dealing, cultural primacy within Europe as a whole clearly belonged to Byzantium; by 1300 primacy was about to transfer its seat to central and northern Italy, where a galaxy of city-states and the restored papacy (after 1378) soon outstripped trans-Alpine Europe as a seat of successful creativity. Even in military matters, the special badge of Frankish prowess, the supremacy of knighthood on the battlefield, was nearing an end by the close of the thirteenth century, when the great frontier boom in the Seine, Rhine, and Thames valleys came finally to a halt.

Before considering this second, 1300–1500, phase of Europe's medieval development, something should be said of the ebb and flow affecting Spanish Islam, Byzantine Christendom, and the steppe cultures of eastern Europe. Spanish Moslem culture and the Islamic steppe culture are usually regarded as non-European, despite the fact that they existed for many centuries on soil that is conventionally defined as part of Europe. This exclusion reflects religious prejudice of very long standing which identified everything admirable with Christianity and abhorred Islam as infidelity. The further fact that Russian and Spanish national sentiment matured in opposition to the Moslem presence on soil that eventually fell to these outposts and guardians of Christian truth, east and west, also colors historical scholarship with often unconsciously preserved, but pervasive, denigration of Islam. When one becomes aware of such bias it is hard not to overreact. My remarks with respect to both Moslem cultures should therefore be understood as extremely tentative.

First, Spain. Moslem Spain achieved a high level of prosperity and civilization in the tenth century. Moslem law dictated full toleration for Christians and Jews, both of which communities played an active part, along with Arabs and Berbers, in the development of literature and learning. Cordova, the capital, rivaled Constantinople in size and magnificence; the Umayyad court consciously and on the whole successfully set out to rival the Abbasids of Baghdad as patrons of art and learning. Conquest by fanatical North African sectarians—Almoravids after 1056, Almohades after 1145—restricted but did not entirely eclipse Spain's intellectual culture, as the life dates and successful public career of Averroës (ca. 1126–98) in Cordova attest. Yet the fanaticism of the Almoravids forced the family of another distinguished Spaniard, the Jew Maimonides (1135–1204), to take refuge in Cairo; and after 1212, when a Christian coalition defeated the Almohade forces in a decisive battle (Las Navas de Tolosa), the great days of Spanish Moslem civilization were over. Yet the three faiths—Christian, Moslem, and Jewish—which had coexisted under the Umayyad caliphs so successfully in the tenth century continued to survive side by side without much difficulty until the fifteenth century.

It is worth wondering why the Spanish bridgehead of Moslem civilization never took deep root in the central and northern parts of the Iberian peninsula and collapsed as completely as it did after 1212. That civilization depended on irrigation agriculture and the dense population such an agriculture could sustain, in much the same fashion that Frankish civilization of northwestern Europe depended on moldboard patterns of cultivation. And just as the utility of the moldboard plow frayed out as one moved eastward, thus setting a limit to the full and free development of the Frankish style of society and culture, so, in all probability, the absence of conditions suitable for irrigation in the northern part of the Iberian peninsula set a limit upon the expansion of Moslem Spanish civilized society. Geographical conditions making cultivation of rain watered land feasible further north were only part, though an important part, of the limitation. Other critical factors were population density, familiarity with the techniques of water engineering needed for building and maintaining irrigation works on a river valley side scale, and, perhaps most critical of all, a military-political system that could regulate and maintain an elaborate system of water distribution and protect the vulnerable water canals from too frequent destruction by hostile raiding parties. After all, if the canals were cut for a mere sixty to ninety days during the critical growing season, complete disaster had to be expected for any population that depended on irrigation. This may well have been what happened after 1212, though irrigation was soon restored under Christian rulers, and the patient labor of Moorish peasants made parts of the sun-drenched, water-shy region around Granada, where Islamic princes ruled until 1492, bloom like a garden even without the waters of the Guadalquivir to feed large scale irrigation works like those that had sustained Cordova in its days of greatness.

An important change in maritime affairs in the Mediterranean also affected the Moslems of Spain adversely. Italian shipping successfully challenged Moslem seafarers in the central Mediterranean soon after 1000. By the end of the century, the Norman conquest of Sicily (completed 1091) made it difficult for Moslem ships to traverse the entire length of the inland sea safely. This tended to cut Spain and the Maghrib off from the main centers of Islamic civilization. The surviving Moslem principalities of the Islamic far west were thus condemned to a more remote and provincial existence than had been the case before. Caravans, of course, remained; but the sea had, for the most part, become Christian, to Italy's great advantage and Moslem Spain's loss.[4]

The decay of Spain as an active center of Islamic civilization was in some measure compensated for through the vigorous development of offshoots from the Spanish stem in North Africa. The geographer and traveler, Ibn Battuta (1304–77), and the great historian, Ibn Khaldun (1332–1406), exemplify this development. Spanish Islam also had a noteworthy afterglow in Christian Europe, where the commentator Averroës, was accorded respectful attention by the doctors of Paris, who discovered Aristotle, for the most part, through translations made in Spain from Arabic versions of his writings. Despite Christian prejudices against Moslems, a few Spanish rulers, chief among them Alfonso X, the Wise (reigned 1252–84), King of Castille, did something to carry on the Islamic tradition of royal patronage of learning. In addition, Arabic verse forms and music stimulated troubadours of Catalonia and southern France to develop a more polished, genteel, and sensual poesy than had been known before in Latin Christen-

4. Shortage of suitable ships' timbers within Moslems' territory was a major reason for their loss of command of the sea. This, in turn, was a result of the failure of Islamic civilization to establish itself securely on well-watered soil until after the year 1000. Their affinity for irrigation-oasis techniques of agriculture condemned Moslems to having to import timber from better watered regions. This put Moslem seafarers at a crippling disadvantage as compared with dwellers on the northern side of the Mediterranean as soon as essential skills of navigation and ship construction established themselves among the Christians of those coasts. Hence, the two main technological weaknesses of Spanish Islam can plausibly be traced back to the fineness of the adjustment Spanish-Moslems made to a semi-desert environment.

dom. Styles of Christian piety and mysticism in Spain also took something from Moslem Sufi traditions, as is particularly evident in the writings of Raymond Lull. Indeed, it is worth wondering whether the distinctive traits that distinguished Spanish Catholicism from that of other parts of Latin Christendom did not owe a good deal to borrowing from, as well as rivalry with, the faith and fanaticism of Islam.

Yet the Christians of the Latin west took only bits and pieces from the Moslem treasury in Spain; the real heir of Spanish Islam was Africa. Indeed, Moslem high cultures in North and West Africa bore much the same relation to Spain as Russian culture bore to Byzantium. There are other interesting parallels between Cordova and Byzantium. The downward curve of Byzantine fortunes and cultural influence that set in toward the close of the eleventh century coincided chronologically with the disasters that descended on Moslem Spain. It is also noteworthy that Cordova and Byzantium succumbed to the same executioners. For just as crusading Christian knights, many of them recent arrivals in Spain from beyond the Pyrenees, damaged the prosperity of Cordova after 1212, so also crusaders from France and Flanders captured and sacked Constantinople in 1204, administering a blow to the economy and society of Byzantium from which the empire never recovered.

Though Latin Christian crusaders therefore had the dubious honor of administering the *coup de grâce* to the high civilizations that had hitherto flourished at either end of the Mediterranean, they were not solely responsible. In Spain, for instance, the Almoravid and Almohade conquerors injected a barbarous Moslem fanaticism into Spanish life that had had disruptive consequences long before Christian fanaticism finished the job. Similarly, Byzantium faced Turkish nomad attackers pressing forward from the east who were almost as dangerous as the Frankish knights and sailors coming from the west.

There is another interesting parallel between what happened in Spain and what happened in Byzantine territory. For just as the Franks damaged a delicate irrigation system in southern Spain and thus made Moslem recovery impossible, so also the advancing Turkish nomads rolled back the frontier of agricultural settlement in Asia Minor and the Ukraine, thereby depriving Byzantine authorities of essential resources which in earlier centuries had permitted the embattled masters of Constantinople to survive as a great and civilized power.

North of the Black Sea, an influx of Turkish tribesmen in the mid-eleventh century damaged whatever agriculture had previously existed on the Ukrainian grasslands and river bottoms. More important, the tribesmen seized command of the strategic areas along the river banks where falls and rapids made it necessary for boatmen to come ashore and use ropes to haul their vessels through the rough water. By intercepting and plundering river flotillas at these vulnerable points, the Turks soon made communication between Byzantium and the Russian lands in the north as precarious as sea communication between Moslem Spain and the eastern Mediterranean was becoming at precisely the same time. Russia, like the Moslem far west, became remote, half cut off from the invigorating fonts of Byzantine culture which had initially nourished the beginnings of civilization in the northern forests.

This Turkish advance across the Ukrainian steppe constituted a severe blow to Byzantine prosperity and security. Far more damaging, however, was Byzantium's loss of the interior of Asia Minor to other Turkish bands. This took place in the decades before and after the battle of Manzikert (1071). As the Turks advanced, agriculture retreated from the broad valleys and upland plateaus of the peninsula. Most of the interior of Asia Minor became a grassland similar to the Ukrainian steppe itself; while the Christian peasantry, which time and again had served as a valuable reservoir of fighting manpower for Byzantium, disappeared. Tax income diminished *pari passu* of course; so did supplies of various raw materials that had traditionally filtered down from the interior to the coastal ports. Without these resources, Byzantium could no longer, as had often happened before, call upon the resources of Asia Minor to repel attack in the Balkans, and vice versa. Since the same foe could not attack both the Balkans and Asia Minor simultaneously, crises on the one front seldom coincided with crises on the other. This had been the great secret of Byzantium's survival; but after about 1100 that possibility had permanently disappeared.

No one knows why the nomads were able to displace peasant cultivators on such a scale. Numbers may have had something to do with the way things went, if it is true that the size of migrating Turcoman hordes that arrived in Asia Minor in the eleventh century were greater than predecessors in earlier times. On the other hand, it is possible that the agriculture and town life of the interior regions of Asia Minor was itself suffering from a creeping crisis, owing to exhaustion of wood supplies. Without a supply of wood for fuel, construction, tool making, and so on, agriculture and city life was literally impossible; nomads had from time immemorial adjusted their habits to an almost total absence of wood supplies. The climate of the interior regions of Asia Minor made forest growth precarious; and increasingly destructive peasant efforts to find enough wood to keep going on traditional lines may have quite literally prepared the way for nomad occupancy by destroying the last remnants of tree growth in one region after another.

Whatever the truth may be about what took place in Asia Minor to undermine Greek Christendom in that region so profoundly, another important change, this one in the regime of the seas, acted against Byzantine interests as powerfully as it did against those of Spanish Islam. For the rise of Italian shipping to dominion over the central Mediterranean meant that the profits of trade gravitated away from Byzantine toward Italian ports. More than that, after 1081 when the Byzantine Emperor accorded the Venetians special exemption from the ordinary excise taxes collected in Byzantine ports, the Greek government lost an important source of revenue and gave the Italians (for other cities soon extorted similar rights from the Byzantines) a crushing trade advantage over its own subjects.

To be sure, the Emperor Alexis I Comnenus (reigned 1081–1118) adroitly exploited the prowess of the Franks who responded to the Papal summons for a crusade in 1097–99 to regain lost provinces in Asia Minor. Some of his heirs worked hard to restore Byzantine defenses, imitating Frankish knighthood and hiring knights from the Latin west in some number. But insufficient cash income restricted what the emperor could do along these lines, and the alternative of infeudation risked fatal insubordination. There was no escape from this dilemma as long as Turkish nomads continued to eat away at the Christian peasantry of Asia Minor and Italian merchants continued to dominate Byzantine sea trade while enjoying exemption from excise taxes. Hence it was a hollow shell that fell in 1204 before the combined forces of Venice and the Frankish knights of the Fourth Crusade.

Yet the economic and political disruption of Byzantium did not lead to cultural decay. First in exile from their capital at Nicaea and then after 1261 restored to Constantinople itself, Greek rulers styling themselves emperors of Rome maintained a brilliant court culture, more self-consciously Greek and more keenly aware of their pagan ancestors than had been the case in earlier ages. Some interesting convergences occurred between the tastes and interests of Byzantine courtiers and those of their contemporaries in Italy, the humanists.

But rapprochement with Papal Christendom, creeping

secularism, and acute concern for elegance of language generated a volcanic opposition among the lower classes of Orthodox Christendom. As a result, in the fourteenth century, impassioned monks, who saw God in mystic visions, won control of the Greek Orthodox Church. The result was to widen and deepen all that separated Orthodox Christianity from Latin Christianity. Yet in asserting their doctrinal and ecclesiastical independence, the monks rejuvenated Orthodoxy and gave the faith a new and powerful missionary impulse. New styles of art and new styles of piety went hand in hand, spreading out from Mt. Athos where monkish mysticism had its headquarters.

The movement penetrated Bulgaria, where pious and learned men devised a standardized Slavonic literary language to propagate their faith. Thence it penetrated westward into Serbia and northward to Russia. In both these lands, new monastic establishments became extremely influential centers from which important aspects of late Byzantine civilization radiated. As in the case of Moslem Spain, therefore, the decay of material power and wealth did not bring an end to cultural influence. On the contrary, it was in the declining days of economic weakness and political upheaval that both Byzantine and Spanish Moslem culture achieved maximal geographic dispersion.

The penetration of a monastic version of Byzantine civilization into Russia and the Balkan interior was facilitated by a notable commercial development that took place in all the lands draining into the Black Sea during the thirteenth and fourteenth centuries. After capturing Constantinople in 1204, most of the Frankish knights soon went home, carrying bits of plunder with them. The Venetians, however, remained and set out to exploit the commercial possibilities of their new position. Before 1204, Byzantine policy had always kept the Black Sea closed to Italian ships. After 1204, on the other hand, the same vessels that sailed the central Mediterranean and Aegean could move also into the Black Sea, penetrating as far as the Don mouth at the head of the Sea of Azov. This meant a vast expansion of the commercial hinterland available to Venice. For a while, disturbed political conditions in the Black Sea region hindered the development of trade; and in 1261 the Venetians lost control of Constantinople, when a *coup de main,* engineered partly by Genoese, restored a Greek emperor to the Byzantine throne. But this setback to the Venetians did not diminish Italian commercial preponderance. Genoese took over where the Venetians had left off; and for the next century these two cities struggled for control of the Black Sea trade. Sometimes they fought all-out wars; more often they resorted to force only on a limited scale or in special circumstances.

What made the Black Sea trade so valuable was this: in the generation after the Italians first broke through into the Black Sea, Mongol conquerors unified and pacified the Russian lands and most of Asia. The Mongol conquest of Russia and the Ukrainian steppes (1237–40) brought a highly efficient administration to that part of the world. Mongol rulers were quite aware of the advantages flourishing trade could bring to their court and armies. In particular, the tribute system they imposed upon the subject Russian principalities mobilized large quantities of furs and other valuables gathered from the northern forests. These the Mongols were eager to trade for the products of civilized workshops—Chinese, Moslem, or European. The Volga served as the natural conduit for the concentration of the Russian tribute, and the Mongols therefore located their headquarters along the lower reaches of that stream. From this center, the rulers of the Golden Horde, as the westernmost branch of the Mongol empire is commonly called, maintained systematic communications with China to the east, Iran to the south, and the valleys of the

Don and Dnieper to the west. Military and political considerations required a highly organized postal system capable of carrying urgent messages at a gallop across the whole of Asia. Lengthy pack trains, toiling more slowly across the same vast distances, served the no less imperative economic needs of the Mongol rulers and their courtiers.

Hence, for about a century, roughly between 1250 and 1350, Italian vessels arriving in Crimea and at other points along the north and east coasts of the Black Sea were able to enter into commercial relations with a vast hinterland extending eastward all the way to China as well as southward into Iran and northward to the upwaters of the Dnieper, Don, and Volga. Genoa was more successful in this trade than Venice, though it was a Venetian, the famous Marco Polo (1254–1324), who left the most vivid and persuasive account of how a bold and resolute man might make his fortune and see the world in the process by venturing along the Mongol trade routes.

After some hesitation, the khans of the Golden Horde officially (and rather tepidly) espoused Islam. With Islam came some of the trappings of Moslem civilization. But nomadic habits and ideals died hard; for a long time the khans shifted their headquarters, summer and winter, migrating up and down the banks of the Volga according to the season. Arts and crafts compatible with the life of mounted warriors certainly flourished among the Mongols; but civilized urban life could have only slender development among a people and at a court that clung tenaciously to migratory patterns of life.

This much is clear: for those who shared the Mongol style of life the charms of settled civilization were insufficient to wean them away from modified nomadry. Pride in their extraordinary military accomplishment reinforced conservatism. In addition, before they appeared in Europe at all, the Mongols had borrowed a good deal from civilized neighbors—

Chinese as well as Moslem. Thus, for example, Mongol administrative, tax, and military systems reflected Ghengis Khan's familiarity with Chinese bureaucratic practice. The Mongols' inclination to reinsure against divine displeasure by adherence to a plurality of forms of worship tantalized Christian missionaries who visited the Great Khan's court in the thirteenth century; but what scandalized and puzzled Christians of the past does not seem irrational or particularly barbarous in an age when we are able, like the Mongols of old, to appreciate some of the charms and reflect upon the rival claims to theological truth advanced by the different civilizations of Eurasia in the thirteenth and subsequent centuries. About art and literature, it is difficult to speak: too much has been lost to allow evaluation, though a few surviving scraps show that by the fifteenth century a thoroughly professional style of painting flourished at Mongol courts on the lower Volga. Like the Mongol administrative structure, this art showed strong Chinese affinities.

Though Mongol high culture was always narrowly restricted, affecting only the court and the yurts of a few notables, Mongols and Italians found it easy to do business with each other. For a century or so, as long as the political unity of the steppe empire held, Italian merchants were able to tap the riches of the whole of Asia through Black Sea ports while also re-establishing a massive southward flow of forest products, grain, fish, and slaves from the Ukrainian and Russian hinterlands of the kind that the Byzantines had monopolized in earlier centuries.

Such a greatly expanded field of trade obviously stimulated Italy's prosperity. Capital accumulated very fast: larger and larger operations became possible. As a result, not long after 1300 nearly all of Europe (and some of Asia as well) came to be tied into a far denser commercial network than ever before. Italian merchants, bankers, and ships, collaborating with the Mongol trade and tribute system, acted as the organizing element of the whole complex. The main sufferers were Orthodox Christians, condemned to pay tribute to the Mongols in the north, and condemned in the south to see the profits of trade and imperial power pass from their grasp and lodge instead in the hands of Genoese, Venetian, and Pisan interlopers.

In the fourteenth century, northwestern Europe was incorporated into the busy Italians' web as well. English sheep farms, Spanish herdsmen, Flemish spinners and weavers all became suppliers of raw material for Italian manufacturers. Sharp eyed financiers and entrepreneurs from Italy organized or reorganized salt mines in Poland, tin mines in Cornwall, alum mines in Anatolia and linked them all into a new, widened trade network from which they profited greatly.

The key breakthrough date for merging the trade and finance of the Mediterranean-Black sea regions with that of northwestern Europe was 1290. In that year, a Genoese sea captain attacked and defeated a Moroccan naval force that had until then closed the Straits of Gibraltar to Christian ships. In the following decades, first Genoese and then Venetian vessels began to ply the Atlantic waters regularly. With the establishment of a dependable maritime connection between Europe's northern seas and the Mediterranean, the superior skill, capital resources, and organization of the Italian merchant communities soon gave them dominant positions in northwest Europe's big business. As a result of Italian enterprise, therefore, in the first half of the fourteenth century, the economies of Spain, England, France, and the Low Countries were incorporated into a truly pan-European market as suppliers of raw materials and semi-finished goods.

Interregional specialization allowed massive import of commodities in short supply locally. In principle, this permitted northwestern Europe to overcome the economic constriction imposed by local food shortages and depletion of forest lands. But it took a while for the necessary adjustments to work themselves out. Men had to move into new occupations and find ways to pay for massive deliveries of grain and timber and other coarse goods from overseas. The Black Death, 1347–51, may have slowed the adjustment. It certainly killed off a very substantial proportion of the inhabitants of northwestern Europe. Population in some localities did not regain pre-1346 densities until the sixteenth century. Hence it was not till after 1500 that northwestern Europe began fully to react to the potentialities interregional trade offered for supplementing its local resources not merely with Italian luxuries, but with articles of mass consumption as well. Before that time, Italians benefited more conspicuously than others from the new pan-European trade patterns, and management of European interregional exchanges remained mainly in Italian hands.

At first glance, the strict discipline of Mongol encampments and the noisy confusion of the city-states of northern Italy seem to have nothing in common. Yet both were able, in very different ways, to mobilize human and material resources for consciously defined goals more efficiently and on a larger scale than had been done before.

The Mongol army and administration was bureaucratic through and through. Men were appointed and promoted to office on the basis of performance; and the test of frequent battle provided a relatively straightforward basis for recognition of merit. Strangers and conquered peoples were fed into the Mongol command system—witness the career of Marco Polo in China—wherever their skills or experience seemed useful. Ghengis Khan and his heirs also appreciated technological improvements, as is shown by their ready resort to gunpowder and other siege weapons borrowed from China.

But generally speaking, the tactics and equipment of horse

archers had been perfected long before the thirteenth century. Technological changes were therefore marginal. The great novelty sustaining Mongol power lay in the realm of bureaucratic command and organizational structures. In 1241 when the Mongol army headed westward, columns advanced on either side of the Carpathians, yet the two maintained regular contact by couriers, so that a single commander could (and did) direct the movements of both forces. Until World War I, no other European commander was able to control such far flung forces or coordinate movements across such difficult terrain. This capacity to communicate and through communication to command and coordinate masses of men at a distance explained both Mongol victories in the field and the cohesion, however, precarious, of the vast empire their victories won.

The upthrust of the Italian city-states—Venice, Genoa, Milan, Florence chief among them—also rested on superior means of coordinating human activity across time and space. But instead of a military command system, run on bureaucratic principles, the Italians relied upon an elaborate network of contractual and corporate relationships that allowed a gifted and lucky individual to make a fortune very quickly and measured efficiency not by success in battle but by capital accumulation. And like the Mongols, the Italian business community developed a keen eye for useful technological improvements, that is, for anything that promised to increase profits or reduce costs.

Indeed, without a far-reaching technical advance in matters nautical the extraordinary thirteenth to fifteenth century expansion of Italian business could not have occurred. Larger ships, steered by stern post rudders, equipped with multiple sails and masts, and decked over against bad weather made it safe to sail the seas at any time of the year. Instead of beaching ships in the fall and launching them again in spring, as had been customary before the thirteenth century, Italian (and other European shipmasters) now kept their vessels at sea all year round, with only such stopovers in port as were necessary to take on and unload cargo, or perchance to wait for a favoring wind or for pirates to go away.

Simultaneously, use of larger containers—for example, barrels weighing a full ton when filled with wine—cheapened the transport of commodities. Handling tuns of wine, like the handling of a heavy rudder or raising a mainsail, depended on mechanical advantage secured through use of block and tackle. Indeed, systematic use of this ancient, simple, and important device for magnifying the power of human muscles probably lay at the heart of the entire nautical revolution of the thirteenth century.

The new ships also needed protection and found it through the development of cross bows. These weapons also magnified human muscle power by using mechanical advantage to bend bows too heavy for a straight pull. A well aimed bolt from such a weapon penetrated armor easily; and when this fact became apparent, the supremacy of the knight in battle ended abruptly—wherever a corps of crossbowmen and the artisan skills needed to produce these weapons in sufficient number existed. This happened suddenly in the Mediterranean when Catalan crossbowmen overwhelmed French knights first at sea, then on land in connection with the fighting provoked by the Sicilian Vespers of 1282. In the more backward lands of northern Europe, the overthrow of knighthood as the decisive element in battle came almost a full two centuries later at the Battle of Nancy, 1477, when Swiss infantry spitted the charging chivalry of Burgundy on a serried array of long-hafted pikes. By bracing the butts of their pikes against the ground, the Swiss discovered a simple and effective way to convert the momentum of a charging knight from a supreme asset into a suicidal liability. Thereby they ended the supremacy of heavy cavalry in northwestern Europe as it had long since been ended in Mediterranean lands by the more sophisticated technology of the cross bow.

Between 1280 and 1330, larger and more seaworthy vessels, protected by efficient missile weapons, spread rapidly through all the European seas. Italians pioneered most, though not all, of the improvements and took the lead in exploiting the new commercial possibilities such ships opened. The critical change was this. Long distance carriage of coarser, cheaper goods became economic. Bulk commodities like raw wool, salt, grain, timber, alum, and iron became worth transporting from one end of Europe to the other, given existing price differentials; and Italian (mainly Genoese and Florentine) businessmen eagerly organized the financial, marketing, and transport facilities needed to make such long hauls pay off. Older exchange patterns involving long distance transport of relatively expensive goods—spices, cloth, luxury manufactures, and so forth—also increased in volume; but the real novelty of the economic pattern woven through all the waterways of Europe by Italian seamen and merchants in the fourteenth to fifteenth centuries was the increased importance of cheap bulk commodities.

Under such a regime, industrial specialization and interregional economic integration opened up all the advantages Adam Smith was later to analyze so persuasively and affected a far larger number of Europeans than had been conceivable before. The marvelous tenth to thirteenth century development of northwestern Europe had been a frontier phenomenon, based on replication in what started as waste forest lands of locally almost self-sufficient communities. Towns with a few square miles of surrounding countryside were the important units in economic matters; politics and war were in the hands of feudal appointees and simple knights, residing in innumerable villages. Links with more distant loci of power were slender, affecting relatively few individuals directly and commanding very little in the way of tax or rent payments to some distant, impersonal authority. With the arrival of cheaper shipping and of Italian entrepreneurial expertise, however, economic integration on a far larger scale grew in importance. Correspondingly, larger political units—whether national monarchies, as in France and England, or the papal monarchy in all Latin Christendom—solidified and extended their control in ways that affected the daily lives of far more human beings than had been possible in earlier times.

The connection between expanded interregional economic specialization and political consolidation was very close. Indeed, the Italians were able to penetrate northwestern Europe economically owing in large part to the protection they had from local rulers, for whom they performed various services in return. Not only could Italians supply luxuries and administrative savoir faire; they also had money to lend. Edward III of England (reigned 1327–77), for example, found it far easier to borrow from Lombard moneylenders than to get his own subjects to pay the costs of his court and of the armies he sent to France to fight what came to be called the Hundred Years War (1337–1453). So much did he borrow from Lombards that when he repudiated his debts in 1339, the news precipitated a first rate financial crisis in Siena, Florence, and other Italian money markets. Financial relations between the papacy and Italian banking firms was even closer; and agents, dispatched from Rome to administer papal revenues in the far corners of Latin Christendom, carried with them much of the business acumen that stood the Italians in such good stead whenever they encountered less commercially sophisticated populations.

At home in Italy, too, the relationship between public authority and capitalist entrepreneur was vital to the economic success that came to the Italians. Cities like Venice and Genoa were governed by men who shared the commercial spirit to the full. Confiscatory taxation was not in question: indeed from many points of view city government was itself managed like a business enterprise. State policy and commercial policy were scarcely distinguishable. Private capital was tapped for public purposes in time of emergency through loans. Interest payments on the Venetian debt were so reliable that subscription to the city's public debt became a favored form of investment for anyone, citizen or stranger, who sought a secure income on his capital. As for Genoa, when the commune fell on evil days financially, most of the powers of government were transferred to what had begun as a private company, the famous Bank of San Giorgio.

Similar self-governing commercial and industrial cities existed in Germany, and in the fifteenth and sixteenth centuries some of them became seats of capitalist enterprise on an important scale. In particular, German businessmen based in Augsburg and other south German towns opened up a series of mining enterprises in central Europe, working eastward from the Harz mountains of Saxony to the mountains of Bohemia and Transylvania. Silver and iron were the most important metals put into circulation through these efforts. Mining technique improved rapidly; deeper and deeper mines were opened, and Germans became the most accomplished miners in Europe—and, for that matter, in the world. A more copious supply of metals and at cheaper cost became thenceforward one of Europe's most important advantages over the other civilizations of the earth.

Further north other German businessmen based in Lübeck and adjacent towns took the lead in developing a new pattern of Baltic trade. As had been true earlier of northwestern Europe, the development of the southern and eastern coasts of the Baltic in the fourteenth to sixteenth centuries depended on the stabilization of a new technological and ecological pattern in what had formerly been a thinly inhabited frontier region. The critical factor was an ample supply of cheap salt, the result, presumably, of discovery and exploitation of salt mines in Poland and elsewhere. With enough cheap salt, herring and cabbage could be preserved indefinitely in brine. As a result, a relatively cheap and nutritious diet—rye bread, cabbage, and an occasional herring on feast days—became available to the population all year round.[5] Salt, of course, had to be paid for. This was managed by developing an export trade in grain and timber—precisely the commodities needed in the older, densely populated lands of northwestern Europe.

Unlike the patterns of life of the tenth to thirteenth centuries, this new Baltic-east European economy required relatively long distance movement of coarse commodities. Salt, grain, and timber, the key items, all had to travel to distant markets. Away from the coast itself, where German merchants took charge, organization of these exchanges fell mainly into the hands of large estate owners or their agents (often Jews). The entire region draining into the Baltic from the Gulf of Finland to the base of the Danish peninsula thus acquired a distinctive social structure in which the landed aristocracy played a far more important managerial role than was true elsewhere in Europe, where, generally speaking, the peasants who actually produced the crop carried their own agricultural surpluses to market and had some discretion about what to sell and when. In the Baltic lands, the peasantry was cut off from these roles. The distant, mass market their labor supplied

5. Rye bread alone lacked sufficient protein and vitamins and could not sustain a healthy population through the relatively long winters of the Baltic regions without supplement. In early times, hunting provided such supplement; but this required a very thin population. The virtue of cabbage and herring was that relatively dense populations could find suitable nourishment from these sources. Incidentally, in western Europe protein-rich beans and peas played a similar role in supplementing the cereal diet available to the common people. These legumes, however, did not flourish in the poorer soils and shorter growing season of the Baltic coastlands.

with grain and timber required larger capital and more elaborate transport than any peasant could command. Hence the neo-serfdom of eastern Europe, that developed *pari passu* with this Baltic pattern of commercial agriculture, was far more oppressive and confining for the peasants than was the case further west.

The Baltic region in turn linked up with the Russian river system through Novgorod. As Mongol power weakened, owing largely to the decay of the bureaucratic rationality that had characterized the Mongol state in its prime, Russian commodities began to flow westward to the Baltic as well as southward toward the Caspian and Black seas. Less was siphoned off by the Mongol overlords; more remained to be exchanged for commodities available through the Baltic trade net.

The upshot of these and other less spectacular developments was to integrate the everyday activity of a very substantial proportion of the entire population of Europe into a single whole, regulated by market relations that focused in a few dozen cities, chief among them those of northern Italy. Strangers living hundreds or even thousands of miles apart combined to produce a result that some businessman, living perchance in still a third locality, planned and intended, though the participants in the process (including the business entrepreneurs) were not necessarily aware of how all the distant and necessary connections were in fact established and maintained.

Until after 1500, Italians remained the chief managers of Europe's interregional economic integration. They were masters of business organization. Partnerships and family scale enterprises were supplemented by state undertakings and by joint stock companies. Some companies became territorial rulers (and plantation managers) in island colonies of the eastern Mediterranean. Indeed, almost all the organizational devices later employed by Dutch and English entrepreneurs to develop trade and industry on a trans-oceanic scale after 1500 were developed first by Italian businessmen who had an empire to exploit within the Mediterranean from the time of the First Crusade until the advance of Ottoman power, 1300–1520, in the east and of Spanish power in the west (climaxed with the unification of Spain under Ferdinand and Isabella, 1492) squeezed the Italians out of most of their managerial roles at either end of the inland sea.

Assuredly, between 1300 and 1500 the capitalist spirit—whether manifested in plantation slavery, accounting techniques, bank credit and cycles of boom and bust, impersonal manipulative use of other human beings, or restless experiment with new techniques, materials, and products—all had ample expression in the great Italian cities of Tuscany and of the Po Valley.

Italy's primacy was never secure, to be sure. Throughout trans-Alpine Europe, local sentiment nearly always disliked the slippery skills Italian entrepreneurs applied so successfully. Whenever local rulers could secure equivalent services from their own subjects, the Italians lost their principal protectors and could expect to be squeezed out. This, in effect, was what happened among the Turks, who found a suitable supply of Greek, Armenian, Jewish, and Moslem businessmen among the populations of the Levant who were capable of performing all the commercial functions Italians had performed along the eastern Mediterranean coasts since 1204 or earlier.

The resulting setback to Italian prosperity was serious. Like the Byzantine empire after it lost control of the interior of Asia Minor, the Italian cities lost the eastern half of their hinterland as the Turks advanced; and after 1453, having seized Constantinople and extinguished the last heir of the Roman empire in the east, the Sultan closed the Black Sea to Italian ships. Constantinople, in short, resumed its former role as imperial mistress and monopolistic market for all the products of the Black Sea coastlands. In the Aegean and (after 1520) Syria and Egypt, Ottoman commercial policy also restricted Italian economic activities very sharply.

Simultaneously, Spain, England, France, and Germany were also pushing back Italian economic influence, partly through state action, partly by the development of local competition. Yet as the scope of Italian economic management decreased, Italian leadership in Europe shifted onto a different plane. For reception of what we know as Italian renaissance culture in trans-Alpine Europe became a really live possibility precisely in proportion as local economic life began to achieve an Italian level of complexity and sophistication. Hence, for a century or more after Italian cities ceased to exercise economic primacy in Europe (roughly after 1500) Italian cultural influence upon the trans-Alpine hinterland continued and indeed increased in importance.

This sort of "ecological" succession may be taken as normal. The spread of classical Greek culture throughout the Mediterranean came after the economic power of Athens and the olive-vine exporting region around the Aegean had broken down. Latin thought and letters penetrated the western provinces of the Roman empire when Italy's economy was already in trouble, thanks to the spread of wine and oil production in Spain and Gaul.

We have just seen how the culture of Moslem Spain and Byzantium began to attract distant peoples more strongly after military and economic disaster had struck the heartlands of both civilizations. Similarly, the diffusion of Gothic art and scholastic philosophy beyond the boundaries of northwestern Europe occurred after the overthrow of the knight's supremacy in the Mediterranean and at a time when the economic transformation of the northwestern forest lands was beginning to reach its natural limits, thanks to the exhaustion of fresh forests to turn into fields.

There is little I need say here about the peculiar qualities of the civilization of the Italian renaissance. Italian writers of the fourteenth century developed an intense admiration for Roman antiquity and a corresponding disdain for both Byzantine and "Gothic" styles of civilization. Such value judgments justified the notion of rebirth that remains embedded in our historical terminology. The politics of northern Italy between 1300 and 1500 did in fact somewhat resemble the struggles among the city-states of ancient Greece; and the development toward monarchical rule (everywhere but at Venice) seemed to recapitulate the political experience of classical antiquity. This was why the study of ancient authors had such importance for Niccolò Machiavelli (d. 1527) and others.

But in most respects, the resemblances between antiquity and the experience of the Italian city-states were superficial, while the differences were profound. The relationship is well reflected in art. Take sculpture, for example, where the influence of ancient models was strongest because numerous antique statues, more or less intact, survived to be studied and admired. Yet any of Michelangelo's (d. 1564) works, his "David," for instance, though it may share such an obvious external as nudity with the art of ancient Rome, nevertheless differed profoundly in spirit and meaning.

If one tries to express the difference between the art of Michelangelo and that of ancient Greece and Rome, it seems fair to suggest that the heart of the matter lies in a kind of self-consciousness that informed the renaissance artist's work. Michelangelo chose a style deliberately: the ancient sculptors knew only one tradition of art and remained within it, not by choice but from ignorance.

This, indeed, seems to me an example of the most important, central, and underlying difference between classical antiquity and the civilization of the Italian renaissance. The Italian world was pluralistic in a far more pervasive fashion than had been true in antiquity. Pagan Rome, so praised by Italians humanists, knew only one model of high culture—that of Greece; and only a small class of rich and powerful men were in a position to share in that culture actively. By the fourteenth and fifteenth centuries, educated men of Europe were at least dimly aware of multiple civilizations, knowing something of India and China as well as of Islam and of pagan antiquity.

More than this, within Europe itself a far greater internal variety and complexity existed. Sharp polarization between a handful of rich—mainly passive receivers of rents and tax income—and the poverty-stricken multitudes prevailed through most of antiquity. This created a far simpler, more brittle, social structure than those of medieval and renaissance Europe. In the latter age, corporate organization proliferated endlessly, all the way from the work group that accompanied each plow team into the fields to the vast corporation of the Latin Church itself. Villages and towns, business enterprises, guilds, military companies, religious orders, territorial governments, estates of the realm, incipient nations, and still other forms of corporate groupings fell in between the professedly universal Church and the humble plow team. Amid such pluralism, overlapping membership was the rule rather than the exception. Conflict and internal frictions were one result of indefinite multiplication of corporate entities, since the interests of one group seldom coincided exactly with those of others, and corporate organization gave increased weight to the will of even the poorer and weaker classes.

Intellectual pluralism was sustained by the corporate complexity of society. Think, for instance, of the rivalry between Dominicans and Franciscans as a factor in diversifying the tenets of scholastic philosophy, or reflect on how Machiavelli and Savonarola coexisted in the same city of Florence, each sustained by a milieu in which his ideas found an appropriate, encouraging resonance. In a society in which corporate structures institutionalized variety as extensively as they did in the major centers of renaissance culture, most men had to make far more, and more important, deliberate choices as to what to believe, how to act, what to do, than commonly occurred in simpler, less pluralistic settings. The self-consciousness we read into the stone figures coming from Michelangelo's chisel says as much to anyone with eyes attuned to the difference between his art and that of the Roman sculptures he studied—and transcended.

By 1500 Europe was well on its way to modernity, if we take the distinctive hallmark of modernity to be pervasive pluralism of society and culture. Centers of economic and cultural dominance within Europe had oscillated sharply since 900, with the rise of northwestern Europe and Russia, the sudden irruption of a Mongol power into eastern Europe, the decay of Moslem Spain and of Byzantium, and the concentration of wealth, power, and creativity in Italy. Yet by the end of the period, weaknesses in Italy's position in Europe as a whole had become evident, with the consolidation of Ottoman, Spanish, and other territorial states. Italian cultural power continued to manifest itself for a century and more; but after 1500 new patterns became important enough to justify taking that date as a major watershed between what are traditionally and appropriately called medieval and modern times.

V
EUROPE SINCE 1500

By 1500, the economic empires created by the city-states of northern Italy were already recoiling before the military power and enhanced administrative efficiency of the Ottoman empire to the east and of the Spanish empire to the west. At the very beginning of the sixteenth century, this power shift entered a critical phase, when both Turkey and Spain built formidable navies, on a scale that far outstripped the material resources available to Venice or any other Italian city. War between Venice and the Turks, 1499–1503, marked the turning point, for it was then that the maritime skill of the Venetians for the first time failed to make up for inferior numbers. Thereafter, within the Mediterranean only the Spaniards were in a position to oppose the Ottomans on anything approaching even terms. The result was a series of naval campaigns, extending from 1516, when Constantinople first extended its naval power to the western Mediterranean with the capture of Algiers, until 1581 when the protagonists made what turned out to be a lasting truce with each other in order to turn attention to more critical frontiers elsewhere.

In spite of sporadic efforts to substitute quality for quantity by pioneering improvements in naval design (for example, the Venetian invention of heavy gunned galleasses that did so well at Lepanto in 1571), the Italian navies were reduced to auxiliary roles in the sixteenth century contest between Spain and Turkey for command of the Mediterranean. An inevitable result of the decay of Italian sea power was the weakening of the mercantile basis for Italian prosperity. The economic hinterland of Venice, Milan, Florence, and Genoa tended to shrink back toward their respective political dominions in northern Italy. Only remnants of their fourteenth to fifteenth century interregional economic domination survived —traffic across the Alps in luxury goods and an export of specialized skills and services to all of Europe whether as bankers, music masters, engineers, architects, or acrobats.

Thus geopolitical roles within the Mediterranean were once more reversed. Spain and Constantinople, whose decay as centers of civilization had permitted the rise of Italy in the eleventh century, became again seats of powerful states and high cultures that were able to overshadow the city-states of Italy by mobilizing far superior resources from vastly larger territories—territories which had, until the administrative consolidation of Spain and the Ottoman empire, acted as important economic hinterlands for the Italians. After about 1500, however, the Italian cities increasingly had to get along on local resources, and ceased to exert dominating influence in anything but the definition of good taste in art, music, manners, and for much of Europe, religion.

This fundamental setback to Italian prosperity was magnified by armed invasion. First the French (1494) and then the Spanish (1502) intruded upon the fair land of Italy, and, having quarreled, precipitated prolonged and bitter warfare. Fighting ended in 1559 when the French recognized Spanish preponderance in the whole of Italy by the treaty of Cateau-Cambresis. For two full generations, the Italian states, which before 1494 had been fully sovereign and accustomed to lead the whole of Europe, suffered repeatedly from pillage and the humiliation of helplessness in face of superior foreign military force. By 1559, those which had not become outright provinces of the Spanish empire, like Naples and Milan, retained precarious independence more on sufferance of the potent foreigners than by virtue of their own strength.

The renaissance spirit that had flourished so strongly in Italy suffered fatal erosion as one after another of the great centers of art and luxury fell prey to plundering soldiers from beyond the Alps. The sack of Rome in 1527 by the army of Emperor Charles V pretty well snuffed out the circle of patrons and artists who had made the papal court the major center of renaissance thought and art in the first decades of the sixteenth century. Thereafter, Venice alone remained hospitable to renaissance attitudes and values, while the rest of Italy soon fell in with a partly Spanish-inspired effort to define and then enforce authoritative religious truth.

The vision of a saving truth, to be served by all right-thinking men with all the force of their being, was in its way just as compelling as the multifaceted vision of human potentiality that had glittered in Italian courts and counting houses at the height of the renaissance. It was in part a natural, necessary, and logical reaction against the inadequacy of the renaissance vision of mankind as maker of his own fate and fortune. For in an age when disaster after disaster descended upon Italy, it was all too obvious that men, whether as individuals or gathered together in cities, did not control their own fate, and were, in fact, playthings of forces utterly beyond their control.

But circumstances pushing Italians and the other peoples of Europe to abandon the individualistic, assertive ideals of renaissance culture and seek instead some authoritative formulation of faith and a reliable routine of piety were far broader than anything happening in Italy alone. In the decades on either side of 1500, a series of rather sharp and sudden disjunctions with earlier patterns of experience struck at Europeans everywhere and in all walks of life. This indeed is what justifies making a new era of European history begin at that time.

First and foremost among these disruptive novelties was the political upheaval that accompanied the spread of cannon and other gunpowder weapons. Indeed, both the rise of the Ottoman state in the eastern Mediterranean and the rapid magnification of Spanish power in its western reaches depended directly upon the gunpowder revolution in armaments. For as soon as cannons became capable of knocking breaches in even the best fortified castles or city walls a few hours after their emplacement, any ruler who controlled a well-stocked artillery park could make his will prevail across comparatively enormous distances. Local defenses had become vulnerable as never before to whoever commanded a few big guns and had the means to carry them to the scene of action (or cast them on the spot, as the Turks did at the siege of Constantinople in 1453).

Aside from strengthening the Ottoman and Spanish empires, the most conspicuous consequence of the gunpowder revolution on European soil was the consolidation of Muscovy in the northeast. The in-gathering of the Russian lands by Ivan III, Grand Duke of Moscow (ruled 1462–1505), and his successor Basil III (ruled 1505–33) created a vast empire which grew to extraordinary proportions because cannons, easily transported by river, gave the Muscovite ruler the means to batter down local defenses of such ancient rivals as Novgorod, Tver, and Pskov with (as least comparative) ease.

Having asserted dominion over all the Russian lands, the Muscovite power next turned its weapons against the remnant of the Mongol empire on the Volga, with the result that by 1557 Ivan IV, the Terrible (reigned 1533–84) extended his reach all the way to the Caspian. Thereafter, Siberia presented no insuperable obstacle. Portaging from one river system to the next, Cossack fur traders and explorers equipped with no more than a few hand guns and their native hardihood, carried Russian sovereignty all the way to the Pacific by 1637. Only the Mongol empire which had preceded it in more southerly parts of Asia and the contemporary Spanish empire of the New World, have ever compared in territorial extent to the Russian empire that thus sprang into being.

In western Europe, however, the weapons revolution of early modern times misfired. The Hapsburg empire of Charles V (ruled 1519–58) looked for a while as though it might provide the kernel around which a state territorially comparable to that of Muscovy or Turkey [1] might crystallize. But Charles V was quite unable to monopolize control of cannons in Europe. Mining and metallurgy had developed so luxuriantly in late medieval times that the critical skills and materials for cannon manufacture were available to European rulers from multiple sources. Elsewhere in the world, relatively slender supply of metal made monopolization comparatively easy. Hence it turned out that local opposition within Germany and Italy, reinforced and frequently fomented by Dutch, French, English, Danish, Swedish, and Turkish efforts to check Hapsburg power, sufficed to maintain a plurality of sovereign states in western and central Europe.

To survive, nearly all European rulers found it necessary to devote enormous effort to equipping armies with cannons and other expensive armaments. Such devices, unused, were liable to rust: hence European rulers were often tempted to engage in the "sport of kings" by provoking war. The upshot was an extremely volatile situation in which Europe's rulers, through their jockeying for wealth, power, and glory, kept society in

1. Not to mention Manchu China, Tokugawa Japan, and Mughal India, all of which consolidated hitherto unequaled territorial dominions by use of cannon.

turmoil. Elsewhere in the civilized world, far vaster states maintained an effective monopoly of heavy weapons in a single hand and did not need to devote nearly so much attention to armament and competitive mobilization of resources for war.

Consolidation of these rival states maintained an unstable and variegated pattern in northwestern Europe. Political divisions tended to reinforce cultural divergences. In particular, instead of continuing to rely on Latin as the common language for learning and administration, as had generally been the case in the middle ages, about a dozen different tongues achieved the dignity of serving as literary and administrative media. Utilization of these mutually incomprehensible literary languages created or, at least, encouraged cultural and intellectual divergences among national groups. On the other hand, within the boundaries of a single state, local differences tended to diminish, though common sovereignty did not always lead to decay of regional peculiarities, as the history of Wales and Ireland after centuries of English rule attests.

The political pluralism of early modern Europe was, I think, fundamental and distinctive. When all the rest of the civilized world reacted to the enhanced power cannon gave to a central authority by consolidating vast, imperial states, the effect in western and central Europe was to reinforce dozens of local sovereignties, each consciously competing with its neighbors both in peace and, most especially, in war. Such a political structure acted like a forced draft in a forge, fanning the flames of rival ideologies and nurturing any spark of technical innovation that promised some advantage in the competition among states.

There was also a most important maritime aspect to the gunpowder revolution. Ships equipped with heavy guns could defend themselves at a distance very effectively. As a result, when European sailors learned just before 1500 to navigate across oceanic distances, their ships proved far more formidable in naval battle than any others afloat. Hence, European intruders, even though few in number and far from home, found it easy to come and go at will, using force or threat of force as a principal stock in trade in dealings with both Asian and Amerindian populations. How effective European naval gunnery could be was demonstrated in 1509 at the battle of Diu (off the west coast of India) where a few Portuguese ships destroyed a far larger fleet without ever allowing their Moslem enemies to bring their numerical superiority to bear by closing and boarding, as traditional tactics in both the Mediterranean and Indian oceans required.[2]

Easy dominion of the high seas lured Europeans, especially those living on or near the Atlantic coasts, to transoceanic adventure. A swarm of explorers, missionaries, and merchants therefore kept on bringing new things to the attention of their stay-at-home contemporaries throughout the sixteenth and seventeenth centuries. By about 1550, trans-Atlantic and other enterprises began to assume real importance; and the scale of European activities—both warlike and peaceable—in the Atlantic, Indian, and Pacific oceans continued to grow thereafter at a rapid rate.

New wealth, information, techniques, and ideas flooded into Europe as a result, and it became increasingly difficult to believe (though most Europeans managed to do so until the mid-seventeenth century) that all important truth had

2. To survive along the stormy shoreline of the North Atlantic, ships had to be built strongly to withstand the shock of wind and wave. It proved easy for such vessels to take the recoil of cannons with no damage. But vessels designed for less stormy seas shook apart after a few shots had been fired. Hence to match European cannonade at sea, a whole new art of shipbuilding had to be acquired; and this no Asian people—not even the Japanese—undertook. Europe's supremacy at sea, 1500–1900, is comparable to the supremacy of knights in land battle, 900–1300, and, interestingly, lasted about as long.

been discovered or revealed long ago to a small segment of mankind. On the other hand, to cut loose from the secular learning of the classics and more especially from the sacred truths of Christianity (or Islam) was more than Europeans could easily bear. Somewhere, somehow, truth and certainty had to be found—or so almost everyone agreed.

On top of everything else, the Spaniards upset the price system of Europe when they opened up extremely productive silver mines in Mexico and Peru. As the supply of silver increased, prices surged upward, since goods did not multiply in proportion to the increase of coins. No one understood what was happening. Nearly everyone believed, as prices rose and traditional economic relationships of all kinds came under new and unprecedented stresses, that the cause of it all had to be evil, greedy men, who somewhere, somehow, were unjustly taking more than was rightfully theirs. Real hardships, inflicted up and down the social scale by laggard readjustments of wage, rent, and tax rates, were thus compounded by a pervasive sense of grievance, though exactly who was to blame could never be agreed upon.

These factors created an extraordinary volatility among European populations. Confronted by too much uncertainty, men sought desperately for some sort of saving truth; and, having found it, commonly set out to enforce its universal recognition. The force and scale of such movements was in turn magnified by the invention of printing (1450's) which made communication of ideas and technical information much easier than before and democratized, if not learning, at least ideology.

Luther's reformation of the Christian church is the archetypical example of this response to the distressing conditions of the age; but there were other comparable movements in every part of Europe. Those that mattered—including Lutheranism—prospered in alliance with political authorities. Indeed, the major states of Europe each became firmly identified with a reformed, purified version of religious truth. Political loyalty and religious conformity tended therefore to be identified, since a subject who adhered to a foreign faith was likely also to prefer obedience to a foreign ruler who had taken that form of faith under his protection.

In eastern and southern Europe, rulers and religious leaders were more nearly successful than in the northwest. In Spain, for example, the identification between emotionally intense Catholicism and the imperial power of Spanish kings led to systematic expulsion of Moslems and Jews from the peninsula. Even converts fell under suspicion, and many of them also fled from fear of the Spanish Inquisition. Muscovy, too, rooted out heresy with fire and sword; in fact, the Grand Duke Basil III (ruled 1505–33) modeled his treatment of the so-called Judaizers on Spanish methods of punishing heresy as reported to him by a Hapsburg ambassador.

The Ottoman empire was different, inasmuch as the Sacred Law of Islam expressly commanded toleration for Jews and Christians who agreed to pay a head tax as a sign of their subjection to Islam. After 1499, however, when an incandescent sectarian challenge to the legitimacy of Ottoman rule flared into sudden prominence in Azerbaijan and adjacent regions, the Ottoman government set out to reinforce Sunni orthodoxy among their Moslem subjects. Overt adherence to rival forms of the faith provoked bloody repression in the first decades of the sixteenth century, but after 1520, when Suleiman the Lawgiver came to the throne (ruled 1520–66), violent persecution gave way to administrative containment and constraint of heterodoxy. Such relaxation was possible because Suleiman's resumption of victorious war against Christendom effectively confirmed the Sultan's claim to legitimacy in the eyes of pious Moslems everywhere.

Yet the sectarian challenge refused to die away. Instead, the Ottoman Sultans had to confront a religious rival on their eastern flank in the form of the Safavid state. The Safavids claimed to be the legitimate successors to the Prophet Mohammed, and as such the sole rightful leaders of Islam. Such a neighbor was more troublesome to the Sultans than their Christian enemies to the west, because war between fellow Moslems, though far from new, still ran profoundly counter to what pious adherents of Islam believed to be right. As champion of the faith against Christian Europe, the Sultans filled a thoroughly congenial and traditionally honorable role. But as champions of Sunni orthodoxy, the same Sultans found themselves quarreling with fellow Moslems with a venom the pious everywhere deplored. Ottoman religious policy therefore remained confused. No simple, radical solution, like those pursued in Spain and Muscovy, was compatible with the complexities of Islamic tradition and the needs of the Ottoman imperial state.

In northwestern and central Europe, religious reformers and political rulers aimed at the sort of religious uniformity that was, more or less, attained in Spain and Muscovy. But the patchwork pattern of political sovereignty that existed in the Germanies meant that religious uniformity could not prevail. Rival rulers, espousing rival versions of the true faith, fought one another to a standstill. Hence, although religious uniformity was imposed within each jurisdiction as a matter of course, in central Europe as a whole, a variegated Lutheran, Calvinist, and Catholic patchwork emerged by 1648, when the sputtering hope of imposing a single truth on all Germans faded away in frustration.

As for France and England, the two largest states of western Europe, both allowed considerable religious dissent, not because kings and prelates were more tolerant, but because nobles and townsmen who dissented from the king's religion were able to organize countervailing forces in both France and England that proved too great for royal agents to overcome. By the time

Louis XIV of France got around to revoking (1685) the Edict of Nantes, whereby his grandfather had guaranteed French Calvinists religious and political privileges, the fierce anxieties that had fired religious controversy in the sixteenth century had begun to dissipate. Consequently, French officialdom stopped short of Spanish and Muscovite rigor in hunting down and punishing the dissenting remnant within France. The English government adopted an explicitly tolerant policy after 1688, partly at least in imitation of Dutch practice.

The Dutch, more by accident than design, made religious toleration pay off spectacularly. The absence of any effective central government among the embattled provinces of northern Netherlands made enforcement of religious uniformity out of the question. This, in turn, attracted persecuted religious groups from most of Europe, many of whom contributed actively to the surge of commercial prosperity that raised Holland to the status of a Great Power early in the seventeenth century. Then, in conformity to a pattern we have learned to expect, as Dutch economic and military power waned (after the 1680's), aspects of Dutch culture, including the policy of religious toleration, recommended itself to increasing numbers of European statesmen and men of letters.

If we try to survey the ebb and flow of events in Europe as a whole between 1500 and 1650 or thereabouts, it is possible to view the discrepant efforts men made to find and enforce a single saving truth as varying forms of reaction against professionalization and ideologcal pluralism (especially as manifested in religious indifference if not outright skepticism) that had come to prominence in Italy during the high renaissance. In Turkey and Muscovy, at any rate, religious reaction started explicitly from rejection of Italian cultural influence in high places. Sultan Mehmet the Conqueror (ruled 1452–80) presided over a religiously tolerant court at which Italian experts offered their services in many different capacities. A pious

Moslem reaction set in after his death, which was soon intensified by court reaction to the Safavid sectarian challenge (1499). As a result later Sultans ceased to patronize secular learning or to employ Italians in posts of trust, relying instead exclusively on skills and ideas available among their own subjects.[3]

In Muscovy, Mehmet the Conqueror's contemporary, Ivan III (1462–1505), opened his court to an influx of Italian influence through his marriage to Sophia Paleologus, who descended from the last of the Byzantine emperors, but was entirely Italian in her education and culture. He imported Italian artillerists, architects, and other experts in some number, and toward the end of his life was suspected of tolerating a court clique of "Judaisers" whose ideas were perhaps also inspired from abroad. Reaction set in even before Ivan's death, when his heir, Basil III, set himself up as protector of Orthodoxy in every jot and tittle. The Orthodoxy he so jealously guarded had already repelled one insidious assault from Italy. For at the Council of Florence (1439) prelates of the Russian church had agreed to union with the Pope, only to be repudiated on their return to Moscow. Thereafter, Russian Orthodoxy came to be identified with punctilious preservation of existing ritual and a deep-seated suspicion of everything alien. It was to this obscurantist tradition that Basil III returned at the beginning of the sixteenth century.

Even in western Europe, the element of reaction against Italian influence was not lacking. The story of Luther's (1483–

3. The displacement of Italian experts from the Sultan's court was facilitated by the influx of Jews fleeing Spain after 1492. Some Spanish Jews had full education in the arts and skills of Christian Europe, and were willing, indeed eager, to put their knowledge at the Sultan's disposal, particularly after their enemy, the government of Spain, became the enemy of the Sultan. Jews acted as experts in residence for all matters pertaining to Christian Europe for about a century, until Greeks displaced them in the mid-seventeenth century.

1546) personal encounter with what he felt to be the scandalous laxity of the papal court is well known; and the volcanic force of his appeal to his fellow Germans rested in part on widespread popular revulsion against the way clever and unscrupulous Italians exploited German simplicity and piety for their own advantage. In Spain, too, the strenuous reform of Catholicism carried through by Cardinal Ximenes (1437–1517) fed upon xenophobia provoked by Italian as well as by Jewish and Moslem activity (especially economic activity) in Spain.

Yet even those who rejected aspects of Italian renaissance culture accepted other sides thereof. Basil III did not throw out the fortification experts his father had imported from Italy, but used their skills to make the Moscow Kremlin one of the most impregnable (as well as one of the most beautiful) strongholds of Europe. Cardinal Ximenes, similarly, patronized the preparation and publication of a famous polyglot Bible that drew upon techniques of philological scholarship that had been perfected among secularly minded humanists of Italy. And German Protestantism, too, in the persons of Philip Melanchthon (1497–1560) and others, incorporated much of the fruit of humanistic learning into the tradition of the Lutheran church, just as Calvin later did for the Reformed churches of Europe and America.

As in many cultural encounters, to reject Italian influence successfully it was necessary to resort to the Biblical tactic of "spoiling the Egyptians," that is, to borrow enough from the foreigners to be able to argue back effectively, whether with words and texts, or with the harsher music of big guns. Different parts of Europe arrived at different compromises between the impulse to throw off corrupting foreign influences and the recognized need to borrow in order to catch up with and overtake the standard set by Italian achievements.

Generally speaking, the reception of Italian taste and learning in France, Spain, and England was relatively broad, presumably because there were substantial groups in the population of those lands that were ready to respond to perceived attractiveness of Italian models, yet were saved from excessive defensiveness by their sense of belonging to a politically powerful state and nation that had nothing to fear any more from Italian economic exploitation. Shakespeare's (1564–1616) free and easy use of Italian plots and settings for many of his plays well illustrates the fruitful relationship such an attitude permitted.

In eastern Europe, comparable groups ready and able to profit from Italian skills were few and weak. As a result, within the pale of Latin Christendom the reception of Italian renaissance culture was more the work of missionaries, based in Rome, than of local elites. The missionary drive got into high gear throughout the Hapsburg and Polish lands in the 1570's and had won over all but a few Magyar gentry by the 1640's. This "baroque" Catholicism brought to Austria, Hungary, and Poland a dogmatically structured version of Italian renaissance culture, as modified under Spanish influence and by Catholic reaction to the doctrinal challenges of Protestantism.

The intellectual and artistic power of this culture was very great. Impressive learning, combining medieval scholasticism with humanistic philology, was marshaled to defend papal definitions of dogma and ritual practice; and the intense conviction with which Catholic (especially Jesuit) missionaries presented such arguments won many waverers to the faith. Schools in which secular, as well as sacred, instruction was intellectually more rigorous than anything previously offered to lay students were an important part of the Jesuit recipe for winning Protestants and other schismatics back to the Catholic faith. The emotional timbre and artistic expression of this culture in music, painting, and architecture were also very powerful. Even sin had its place. A heightened ideal of sexual repression, applicable to laity as well as to clerical personnel, found its complement in the license of carnival; and the confessional offered a ready remedy for practically any personal shortcoming.

So powerful, in fact, was the appeal of baroque Catholic culture that Orthodox Christians in the Balkans and Russia could not escape its attraction. Early in the seventeenth century, Greek prelates in Constantinople and other centers launched their own campaign to "spoil the Egyptians" by importing into the Greek world a version of Italian higher education. Preserved and elaborated within the Venetian dominions, this learning had the double virtue in Greek eyes of being Aristotelian (and therefore in a sense their own, merely reappropriated after a lapse of centuries) and anti-papal (for the Jesuits had been unable to modulate the scientific rationalism that dominated the University of Padua in the sixteenth and early seventeenth centuries). The result was that during the ensuing century a few strategically placed Greeks received a rigorous scientific education and became thoroughly familiar with contemporary Italian culture. Such men, beginning in 1669, acted as diplomatic agents for the Turks (who had ceased to pay attention to new winds of doctrine or even to new technologies originating in Christian Europe) in all dealings with the Sultan's increasingly formidable enemies in the west.

Muscovite reaction to the challenge of papal Catholicism was stormy. Educational upgrading at Kiev and elsewhere made it clear that Russian Orthodoxy was not everywhere the same. Minor variations in ritual had somehow crept in, but local peculiarities had warm support from pious and dedicated men, who saw in any change, even the most trifling, an evidence of the abandonment of Orthodoxy. In such a situation, the only logical way to decide what was truly Orthodox was to consult Greek texts of the church fathers and decrees of early Councils. But this, it soon became clear, meant some changes in Russian practices; and many Russians, the so-called "Old Believers," refused to accept the logic that compelled others to undertake official reform and standardization of ritual. The result was a profound schism in the Russian church.

By forcing all those most attached to unchanging Orthodoxy into the ranks of the Old Believers, the schism in effect paralyzed resistance to a further wave of technical modernization launched by Peter the Great at the end of the seventeenth century. Tsar Peter (reigned 1689–1725) could afford an almost complete disregard for Orthodox sensibilities because so many Old Believers had already begun to expect the Second Coming of Christ to set things right in a world where the approaching apocalypse was clearly attested by the apostacy of the very men—Tsar and Patriarch—whom God had appointed to protect the one, true Orthodox Christian faith.

By the time Peter the Great came to the throne of Russia, however, Italy had ceased to be the main center of European cultural creativity. Both renaissance pluralism and Baroque Catholicism had spent their force, being incorporated into the cultural inheritance of trans-Alpine and eastern Europe in greater or lesser measure. Instead, a new center had defined itself in northwestern Europe, occupying almost exactly the same territorial heartlands as had the Frankish civilization of the tenth to thirteenth centuries. The change was symbolized by the fact that when Peter decided to visit the west he headed for Holland and not for northern Italy, as a man on a similar mission would certainly have done two hundred or even one hundred years before.

What happened to bring this fundamental shift about? First, and most obvious: Italy and all other Mediterranean lands confronted crippling economic crisis at the beginning of the seventeenth century. Population growth outran local food production; and the problem was compounded by widespread destruction of woodlands. Plague and other forms of disease of course brought population quickly into line with available food supplies; only in exceptional circumstances were Mediterranean cities able to pay for grain imported from the Baltic, as happened briefly but dramatically in the 1590's. However, restoration of a precarious food-population balance did nothing to bring back an adequate wood supply. Fuel, therefore, became scarce and expensive, handicapping shipping and industry of almost every kind. The Mediterranean lands have yet to recover from this setback. Early in the seventeenth century, both large-scale commerce and large-scale industry deserted the crowded shores of Europe's southern sea. Only the development of continent-wide electrical power grids in the second half of the twentieth century promises to redress the fuel shortage handicap under which Mediterranean Europe has had to labor ever since the latter sixteenth century.

To be sure, neither Spain nor the Ottoman lands were as densely populated as Italy, and some obvious possibilities—irrigation agriculture for example—could have raised the food producing capacity of Spain and European Turkey enormously. But social conditions did not reward peasant industriousness sufficiently to make the heavy investment such cultivation requires attractive; and neither government officials nor private landlords had the technical knowledge and entrepreneurial imagination to marshal the requisite peasant labor by force. Instead, barren hillsides and treeless plains attested ecological disaster, brought on and perpetuated by political conditions and human patterns of work and property as well as by brute pressure of population—human, sheep, and (not least) goat.

The social effect of the Mediterranean food and fuel crisis was to depopulate cities and pond back underemployed masses of people in the countryside. There, at least, hungry mouths were close to whatever food there was. Poverty, ignorance, idleness multiplied under such a regime. Undernourished, unskilled peasants dominated society by sheer weight of numbers. Everything that had made Italy and the Mediterranean the center of European civilization weakened and faded away, not least intellectual and artistic creativity.

Pervasive poverty certainly hurt Italian, Spanish, and Ottoman high culture from the seventeenth century onward. Diminishing means restricted opportunities of all kinds. Yet poverty by itself does not seem an adequate explanation for the suddenness of Italy's intellectual collapse. In 1609–10 when Galileo Galilei (1564–1642) turned his new invention, the telescope, to the skies and announced startling astronomical discoveries week after week to all the world, the University of Padua, where he was then a professor, was also the leading center of medical study in Europe. Twenty-five years later, Galileo was under house arrest for failure to heed an earlier ecclesiastical warning against the heretical notion that the earth revolved around the sun, and the great days of Paduan science were gone forever, as new centers rose north of the Alps to attract students and teachers of the caliber that had once made Padua famous.

What happened was this: the very success with which Roman Catholics of the sixteenth century carried through their effort to chart the entire universe and define man's place in it created an authoritative doctrine which collided unyieldingly with new data and new ideas at the beginning of the seventeenth century. The completeness of the moral-intellectual systems of truth, generated both by baroque Catholicism and by official Ottoman Islam had paradoxical results. Authoritative and relatively unambiguous answers to all important questions were what men wanted and what these systems provided so convincingly. Herein lay their strength, an essential aspect of their appeal to troubled minds. But on the principle that a chain of reasoning, like a chain of iron, is no stronger than its weakest link, completeness also created radical weakness. Dissent on any point automatically called the authority of the entire belief system into question. After all, the same authorities and the same procedures for determining truth guaranteed each and every doctrine and prescribed behavior. Hence since theological experts declared that the sun went round the earth, evidence and arguments to the contrary, no matter how persuasive, had to be denied, as Galileo discovered to his distress in 1616 and again in 1632.

Under such circumstances, a wise and prudent man refrained from expressing doubts, even to himself, and instead sought out a niche, ready prepared within the system of belief and conduct, where he could be reasonably comfortable. Thus heirs of such rich and coherent intellectual traditions, whether Moslem or Christian, usually persuaded themselves that intellectual conformity and reverent respect for established truths was morally right and necessary. Broadly educated, intelligent, and sensitive individuals, who under other circumstances, might have taken the lead in developing new ideas, were exactly those who comprehended best the delicate interdependence of the entire belief structure, and who were therefore most eager to defend it against narrow, irreverent specialists like Galileo. Moreover, Galileo's novel and heretical opinions were based on physical and astronomical observations which, depending as they did on faulty and imperfect human senses, were intrinsically liable to error. Careful deduction from first principles seemed logically far more secure; all the more when such deductions supported (or at least harmonized with) sacred religious truths.

No doubt economic and intellectual conditions of Mediterranean lands in the early seventeenth century acted subtly one upon another. Had economic circumstances not been so constricted, perhaps conformity to dogmatic authority in matters intellectual would not have been so pervasive; conversely, if pious explanations and religious remedy for economic hardship had not been so impressively at hand, men might have searched harder for economic and political alternatives. But as things were, economic constriction and the hardening of dogmatic definitions of permissible belief advanced simultaneously in Spain, Italy, and Ottoman lands. Artistic creativity lasted longer, particularly music (Turkish as well as Italian), which, being innocent of definite doctrinal meaning, escaped even the most officious efforts at thought control.

The impasse confronting Mediterranean Europe in the seventeenth century was all the more conspicuous because at about the same time two other regions of Europe were beginning to enjoy the advantages of a rapidly expanding economy. In the northwest, Holland, England, and France embarked on successful trans-Atlantic colonization soon after the turn of the century; and all three nations made substantial gains in the Indian Ocean as well. With the decay of Spanish and Portuguese energies, these northerners moved in and started to take a far more aggressive part in settling North America, exploiting India and the Spice Islands, developing sugar plantations in the Caribbean, and in other ways pursuing and expanding economic empire overseas. Techniques for organizing overseas enterprises which in the fourteenth century had been an important part of the Italian secret of economic dominance—stock companies, plantation management, financial accountancy, and so on—had become fully domesticated in the north by 1600. They were put to work by Dutch and English businessmen with the same brilliant success that had earlier come to businessmen of Genoa and Florence.

Two important technical developments sustained the upsurge of northern wealth in the seventeenth century. One was agricultural: Dutch and English farmers of the seventeenth century, by systematic experiment and a good deal of trial and error, discovered how to get along without fallowing. Fallowing one third or more the arable land each year had been fundamental to traditional moldboard cultivation. It kept the plow busy in summer months when the grain was ripening; more than that, it was an effective way to destroy weeds, which would otherwise have accumulated in the soil so thickly as to crowd out the grain. The same result, it was discovered, could be achieved by hoeing ground planted with turnips. Turnips could then be fed to stock in the wintertime, allowing the farmer to support more and stronger animals than the traditional method had permitted. An alternative was to plant alfalfa or some other leguminous crop; it too provided fine winter fodder, kept back weeds by its early, vigorous growth, and simultaneously enhanced fertility for the next year or two by depositing nitrogen in the soil. These and related improvements (for example, in the design of plows, mechanical seeders, and harrows) allowed the production of more food per acre and per agricultural laborer than had been possible before. A corollary was that a larger per cent of total population became available for tasks unrelated to food production.

Fuel shortage of the sort which hit the Mediterranean so hard (and which may have been partly or even largely responsible for the set back to northwest European prosperity in the fourteenth century) was solved even more decisively by the growing exploitation of coal. England had particular advantages here, because easily exploitable coal fields existed immediately adjacent to navigable water at Newcastle and other places in the Tyne estuary. These mines were very conveniently located with respect to London and other North Sea ports. Timber, especially oak suitable for shipbuilding, remained in critically short supply and had to be jealously guarded. Moreover, until the eighteenth century, coal could not be used to smelt iron because sulfur and other chemicals from the coal entered the iron and made it uselessly brittle. For that reason Sweden and distant Russia became major iron producers since their forests provided an ample supply of charcoal at a time when western Europe had depleted its forest resources to a point that made smelting difficult. Coal was therefore not a perfect substitute for wood. Nevertheless, it relieved most of the problems which crippled industry in the Mediterranean, and allowed the coal-rich north to use the labor released from the task of raising food for a wide variety of new industrial (and commericial) activities.

With food and fuel supplies thus more or less satisfactorily assured, northwestern Europe was in a position to take over the dominating economic role north Italy had formerly played vis-à-vis the rest of the continent. Raw materials in scant supply at the center could be and were imported: grain, timber, and iron from the Baltic or from the North American colonies were supplemented by new or newly important commodities such as sugar from the Caribbean, tobacco from Virginia, cotton from India, tea from China. Naval supremacy, resting first with the Dutch, and, after 1688, with the English, backed up commercial domination of oceanic routes as well as of Europe's coastal waters, including the Mediterranean.

England's insularity was particularly advantageous, for control of the narrow seas along the English coasts made elaborate investment in land defenses unnecessary. Parliamentary parsimony in appropriating funds for public purposes meant that wealth could and did increase more rapidly than taxes, benefitting private enterprises and persons and allowing accumulation of capital in the hands of men of quite modest circumstances. At the top of the social scale, the rich, too, got richer, sometimes spectacularly so by profiting from increments of land value or by speculating on large-scale ventures far afield. A wealthy aristocracy and business oligarchy on top of a numerous population of shopkeepers and professional men thus took shape in Great Britain, giving English society a distinctive, middle-class bulge which lasted into the twentieth century.

These solid successes in the northwest were matched by a

large scale frontier boom in the east. Until the seventeenth century, the steppe lands of the Ukraine, Rumania, and Hungary remained open grass, occupied by grazing herds and a few men tending them. Cultivators had been unable to survive, even in the most promising soils, because of slave and booty raids launched at frequent intervals by Tartar horsemen. The Tartars were remnants and heirs of the once formidable Mongol empire, based, after 1557, only in the Crimea and protected, in a vague way, by the Ottoman Sultan.

Tartar depredation depended on finding the frontiers of agricultural settlement poorly defended. As hand guns became available in greater numbers and as a better organized military establishment took form in Austria on the one flank and in Muscovy on the other (Polish armies, while sometimes formidable, were never well organized), the balance slowly but surely tipped against the Tartars. Settlers advanced, by trickles at first, later in a flood. After 1667, when Russia annexed most of the Ukraine, and 1699, when the Hapsburgs asserted control over most of Hungary, the eastward movement came firmly and finally under the direction of official bureaucracies of the major east European states.

Even the Turks, though driven from Hungary and the Ukraine, were nonetheless able to open the Rumanian grasslands to cultivation on a wholesale scale. This in turn allowed Ottoman officialdom to feed Constantinople adequately once more, for Rumanian grain exports could be paid for handsomely with monies collected as tax and tribute from the Christian (after 1711 Greek) rulers whom the Turks appointed to govern the province. The food problem that had troubled Constantinople, like all the other big cities of the Mediterranean at the beginning of the seventeenth century was thus triumphantly solved in the latter part of the same century. Ottoman armies, likewise, achieved a new lease on life thanks to the availability of a much enlarged food supply. The so-called Küprülü revival of offensive war against Crete, Russia, and Austria, climaxing in the second, unsuccessful Ottoman siege of Vienna in 1683, would not have been possible without the massive development of Rumanian agricultural resources.

Generally speaking, the pioneers who broke the sod in southeast Europe were poorly equipped and careless husbandmen. But wide stretches of the steppe were ideally suited by nature for the raising of wheat. Hence, even technically sloppy cultivation often produced fine harvests; and the cheapness of transport by river made it possible to market Ukrainian grain in distant cities. From 1667 or before, the increasing grain harvest produced along Russia's southern frontier fed Russian soldiers and state officials as well as iron workers in the Urals and other less important industrial work forces elsewhere. This allowed very rapid development of Russian state power, since the river network made delivery of grain (and other commodities) across long distances a practical proposition. After 1774, when Russian ships gained the right to travel freely through the Turkish straits and enter the Mediterranean, massive exports from Odessa and other Black Sea ports provided an additional outlet for the mounting production of Ukrainian grainfields. Russian grain thus became available to Mediterranean populations on such a scale and at a price that significantly relieved the chronic food shortages that had afflicted Mediterranean city folk since the latter decades of the sixteenth century.

Obviously, the spectacular frontier development of Russia overland and of northwestern Europe overseas put the intermediary regions of the continent under special pressure. Poles and Swedes, though they participated in the early stages of the frontier development in the east (Poland agriculturally in the Ukraine, Sweden in timber and iron production) failed to organize state power strong enough to cope with the Muscovite autocracy. In the eighteenth century, both these states therefore became little more than Russian puppets. Many German states descended to the same status vis-à-vis Germany's western neighbor, France. But Prussia and Austria managed to mobilize sufficient resources from local populations to sustain an army and supply system that made those states, like England, France, and Russia, rank as great powers by the middle of the eighteenth century.

Prussia's secret was superior administration and a distinctive ruthlessness in subordinating private and corporate interests to the overriding needs of the state. The harsh memory left by the Thirty Years' War (1618–48), when Prussian land had been plundered for years on end by occupying foreign troops, provided the initial stimulus to the development of Prussia's militarized administration. Austrian state power benefited from its role as principal guardian of Christian Europe against the Turks, for corporate and private resistance to paying taxes or rendering services in war against the infidel was noticeably less than when the emperor sought means with which to fight fellow Christians.

Generally speaking, the increase in the Russian state's resources through frontier development and the increase of Austrian and Prussian state power through intensified administrative manipulation more or less kept pace during the seventeenth and eighteenth centuries. Otherwise expressed: deficiencies of Russia's administrative articulation and defects of Russian technical skills offset the superior geographic and demographic base upon which Russian state power rested. But during the reign of Catherine II the Great (1762–96) Russia began to catch up with her western neighbors in technical and administrative matters, and definitively outstripped the Turks.

The resulting upthrust of Russian power threatened to upset the existing fivefold great power structure of interstate relations. This was not the first time such a thing had happened in Europe, for just a century before Catherine's Russia waxed so mighty, the consolidation of the French monarchy under Louis XIV (reigned 1643–1715) had also threatened to upset Europe's balance of power. But Louis' initial superiority was eventually contained by a Dutch-English-Austrian alliance, though not until long drawn out struggles against the French had strained Dutch resources to the limit and undermined the commercial dominance Amsterdam had enjoyed at the beginning of the seventeenth century.

The repeated adjustments of the international balance of power in the seventeenth and eighteenth centuries through war and diplomacy was, indeed, a minor triumph for rationality and calculation in human affairs. Far more important for European civilization as a whole was the way rulers and administrators rationalized the application of violence by bureaucratizing armies. The principles were age old: in the seventh century B.C. ancient Assyrian kings set up regular career promotion patterns for their army officers and paid them enough, in booty and otherwise, to make the career attractive. Roman and Byzantine imperial administrators had likewise been familiar with the concept of a standing army, commanded by officers, appointed, paid, and promoted by the emperor or his delegated agent. The Italian cities in the late fifteenth and sixteenth centuries also supported professional military establishments, but few city administrations, except the Venetian, had enough cash and enough continuity of purpose and policy to create a permanent professional force of trained men, available winter and summer, in peace as well as in war.

Military professionalism instead took a mainly private form. From the time of the Hundred Years' War (1337–1453) (and sporadically before) self-appointed military entrepreneurs set out to raise a troop or company and offered their services to whoever had means to pay. As long as Europe's rulers could not afford to support large military establishments on a permanent basis, this arrangement continued to prevail, for it offered the possibility of putting comparatively large and well-equipped forces in the field on short notice. On the other hand, a successful captain was likely to try to seize power for himself, as the careers of many Italian *condottieri* of the fourteenth and fifteenth centuries demonstrated. Short of this, even if dismissed with all arrears of pay settled, discharged soldiers were liable to plunder their former employers' subjects, especially if the onset of peace threatened them with unemployment. Calling upon mercenaries could therefore become far more costly than anything provided for in the initial contract.

This fact burnt itself into the minds of Europe's rulers in the course of the Thirty Years' War, which devastated much of Germany, 1618–48. In the early stages of that struggle, private military entrepreneurs enjoyed unparalleled opportunity, and the scale of their armies exceeded anything known before. But by 1634, Emperor Ferdinand II felt his power threatened by Albrecht von Wallenstein, the most successful captain in his service. The emperor succeeded in first dismissing and then concurred in the assassination of his overmighty ex-employee. Thereafter, all Europe's major rulers devoted systematic effort to assuring soldiers' loyalty and obedience. They reduced military entrepreneurial commands to the relatively small scale of a single regiment and endeavored to surround the contract for military services with a semi-sacred aura by assimilating it to the ancient feudal oath of homage and fealty which knights had once offered to their liege lords.

Moreover, when the war ended, the rulers of France, Austria, and other major European states maintained a few regiments on a standby basis, as much to overawe potential rebelliousness at home as to guard against foreign threats. Little by little, promotion, pay, and other perquisites of the officer class came to depend less on the colonel of the regiment and more on the decisions of some clerk in the central offices of government. Simultaneously, systematic efforts were made to ritualize and reinforce solidarity between monarchs and the officers of the army. Kings began to wear military uniforms on all sorts of public occasions; royal parades and reviews multiplied; young officers were assigned decorative and ritual function at court; royal princes were often raised as cadets, and so forth. The result was extremely successful. Unruly aristocrats of past ages enrolled their sons in the new armies gladly enough; private war and local rebellion, which had remained an ever present reality of European politics through the sixteenth and early seventeenth centuries, ceased to be a live possibility, save in remote fringe regions like the Scottish Highlands (risings, 1715, 1745), eastern Hungary (risings 1703–11), and the Don-Volga frontier (rising 1773–75).

The French army quickly became the most powerful and best administered of Europe. Ministers who spent their lives nursing the royal income to make it capable of sustaining the cost of court and army quickly came to the conclusion that a plundering soldiery was too expensive to be endured. Plundering reduced the tax value of land through which the army had passed for years afterward, and made annexations of devastated territory scarcely worthwhile from a fiscal point of view, at least until after years of peace had allowed gradual recovery. In addition, plundering took men away from the field of battle and weakened discipline. Hence, it became royal policy to supply the French armies with food and other necessities from magazines located along the route of march. This limited mobility; on the other hand, it made war worthwhile, at least as long as the French faced weaker forces in the field, as was true, generally speaking, until 1689. By then the French policy and the reasons for it had become general—

in principle if not always in practice—among Europe's Christian princes. Only the Turks adhered to the older custom of allowing irregular troops to plunder almost indiscriminately, within as well as beyond the Ottoman frontier.

From the point of view of the ordinary subject, no matter how burdensome taxes required for the support of a regular army might be, they were nonetheless preferable to risking ruin at the hands of marauding soldiery. Overall, the result was a significant reduction of the incidence of violence in most Europeans' lives. At the same time, the controlled, deliberate application of force on the field of battle increased in scale and effectiveness as trained men, using carefully thought out tactics and equipped with weapons designed and redesigned in the light of battle experience, confronted one another at frequent intervals in obedience to the will of their kings and commanders.

Nor were the triumphs of early modern military administration merely rational. Close order drill, like the drill of the ancient Greek phalanx or the training necessary to allow Swiss pikemen to keep their place in maneuvers, had powerful psychological effects upon soldiers subjected to endless repetition of prescribed movements, performed in unison. Such movements had rational purpose of course. Properly done, they assured that soldiers kept formation in march and deployed rapidly to maximize fire-front on the field of battle. Even more important, with sufficient training the complicated movements required to load, aim, and fire a musket could be performed reliably and in minimal time by every soldier, despite the confusion and excitement of battle. Moreover, endless practice kept idle hands busy, even in winter time.

But military drill also had a profound and entirely subrational payoff of which European monarchs and their drill masters were either unaware or took so much for granted as not to bother mentioning it. Nevertheless, anyone who has taken part in the by now empty ritual of twentieth century close-order drill will reognize that marching men, moving in unison for prolonged periods of time, develop a strange and remarkable emotional rapport with one another. Those who as young men have never marched find it hard to believe that a visceral sense of solidarity with everyone else participating in this sort of activity arises as powerfully as it does. The fact is that such behavior probably stirs echoes of men's earliest sociality. Modern close-order drill seems capable of summoning back to life the shades of ancient hunting bands, whose members must have danced around the camp fire before and after the hunt, moving in unison, building up a spirit of camaraderie and creating courage in the face of anticipated danger by collective incantation, expressed both by voice and gesture. Countless European drill sergeants achieved comparable results, despite the fact that they usually started with extremely unpromising human material.

Taming the human penchant for violence by such sleight of hand and putting it under rational bureaucratic management surely deserve to rank among the more remarkable achievements of Europe's Old Regime.

Proof of the power accruing to European armies through these training and administrative practices was their success in wars with other peoples. Within Europe itself, Christian armies clearly outclassed the Ottoman Turks and the nomads of the steppe before the end of the seventeenth century. In the eighteenth century, India, too, proved unable to resist even the slender European forces that could be deployed across oceanic distances. But in the Far East, the military establishments of imperial China and imperial Japan were still able to hold Europeans at arms' length. Nowhere else in the entire world was there a force capable of resisting the armies that European states maintained as a matter of course.

In matters of art and intellect, the professional autonomy

of specialists, which had attained such substantial development among the Italian cities of the high renaissance, never disappeared, even when the drive to cage all truth in a single authoritative formula was at its apex. It was, not unnaturally, in the parts of Europe where governmental authorities met with least success in establishing and enforcing a pattern of total truth that professional autonomy best survived and began again to flourish and proliferate soonest. Holland became hospitable to the sort of intellectual pluralism characteristic of the renaissance before that spirit faded from Venice, its last place of refuge in Italy, about 1630. René Descartes (1596–1650), for example, prudently took up residence in Amsterdam and cautiously waited to see just what might happen to Galileo before venturing in 1637 to publish the first fruits of his own scientific and philosophical researches, whose compatibility with Catholic doctrine he carefully affirmed but did not care to test by living in an officially Catholic country such as his native France.

In 1660, the restoration of Charles II to the English throne precipitated a powerful revulsion in England against the Puritans' effort to constrain human life to an authoritative interpretation of God's will. The result was to give free rein to a broad variety of life styles and professionalized activity—whether on the stage, in private conduct, or in investigation of how to improve tillage, measure gas pressure, or unravel the mystery of the universe with the help of ecstatic visions. New communications nets sprang up to connect kindred spirits. These ranged all the way from George Fox's (1624–41) Society of Friends (or Quakers), formally organized in 1669, to the Royal Society of London, founded in 1660, whose published *Transactions* quickly became a means of conveying new data, stimulating new researches and exciting new thoughts among a wide circle of subscribers.

Similar societies arose in other European countries, though

Catholic governments did not usually permit religious fellowships like the Quakers to flourish freely. Counterparts of the Royal Society of London, however, became fashionable throughout Europe, many of them endowed or founded by kings and princes who were eager to win fame as patrons of learning. Such societies exchanged publications with the Royal Society and with each other; in addition, a vigorous private network of correspondence allowed Europe's leading scientists, mathematicians, and philosophers to exchange news and views of professional interest, wherever they might happen to be living at the time. These new patterns of communication stimulated natural science so that it began to flourish as never before. A community of inquirers and experimenters spread across Europe as far east as St. Petersburg and across the oceans to distant Philadelphia and Lima. The major centers of scientific research remained, however, in England, France, and Holland, where social structures, educational establishments, and increasing wealth all helped to sustain such activities.

The great monument of the age was Isaac Newton's (1642–1727) radically simple mathematical analysis of the behavior of moving bodies, whether celestial like earth, sun, and moon or terrestrial like cannon balls and falling apples. By bringing all such cases under the same formulas, Newton broke through, once and for all, the separation traditional European physics had made between things celestial and things of this earth. The blow to older, theologically certified views was correspondingly severe; and yet the demonstrated accuracy of Newton's formulas, tested over and over again both by astronomical observations and by ballistic research, could not be easily dismissed by anyone who understood the argument. Newtonianism therefore spread; and as it did so, radical adjustments in religion had to follow.

Characteristically, a religion of the heart, eschewing dogmatic and doctrinal definition and seeking personal holiness through private devotions, could accommodate Newtonian science easily enough, by simply sloughing off astronomical and other beliefs Christians of earlier times had accepted but which were now proven erroneous. In parts of Europe where such pietistic traditions were already strong, the "Enlightenment" arrived in the eighteenth century without interfering too much with religious faith and practice. This was the case in Protestant Germany and also in England. Where such movements had been officially suppressed, as in most of Catholic and Orthodox Europe, however, the Enlightenment collided head on with a hardened carapace of ecclesiastical doctrine. Eventually, it was the ecclesiastical carapace that cracked, giving way, in many instances, to some form of radical unbelief, whether deism or atheism.

Political and economic theory, history, drama, and *belles lettres* all flourished exceedingly too; and once again the most influential writers clustered mainly in England and France, with Dutchmen and Germans sometimes important. The same countries took the lead in painting, though Italy's fame as a center of the visual arts was not entirely eclipsed by the rise of Dutch and French schools. Music was different, for in that domain, Italian creativity lasted into the eighteenth century; and when musical primacy shifted north of the Alps, it was Germany, particularly Catholic Germany, that took the lead in creating what by the nineteenth century was already called "classical" music.

The custom whereby the music of the eighteenth century is called classical is suggestive, for there is a sense, surely, in which the entire social and cultural universe developed in Europe by the early decades of the eighteenth century was potentially "classical." That is to say, subsequent generations might have accepted as normative for all true civilization the balances of the early eighteenth century within society and between states, together with rules agreed upon by all important artists and thinkers, for applying rational and conventional checks to raw human impulse.

But in fact, of course, it was Europe's fate to become the scene of further revolutionary upheavals. The collapse of the Old Regime in France in 1789 signaled the collapse of the eighteenth century pattern of European society and civilization and launched the continent on yet another chapter of its stormy history.

The revolution in France had such importance partly because the aspirations summed up in the slogan "Liberty, Equality, Fraternity" were widely shared in Europe of the day, and beyond Europe's confines in the Americas, too. Indeed, the American Revolution preceded and helped to precipitate the great revolution in France; similarly, there were important and energetic groups in the Belgian, German, and Italian populations—not to mention Poles—who received the French as liberators, even when they came with arms in hand, and began to requisition supplies left and right from liberated and/or conquered neighboring peoples. The force of such responses to revolutionary ideas and practices meant that most of the changes the revolution brought were irreversible, even when men deeply opposed to revolutionary ideals came to power after 1815.

Ideology and its appeal was not the only reason for the revolutionary success. By sweeping away innumerable corporate privileges and local monoplies on positions of power and pecuniary reward, the revolutionaries created careers open to talent. Men of unusual capacity came from "nowhere" and made their fortunes—whether in civil life or in the ranks of the army. This meant, of course, that all who rose rapidly in social status became defenders of the revolution. Being fully conscious of their individual and collective interest in preventing the reassertion of old privileges and monopolies, the newcomers easily outweighed those who had profited from the arrangements of the Old Regime, even when restoration became the slogan of the day.

Finally, the reorganization of society and public administration that the revolutionaries carried through increased the capacity of European governments to mobilize men and resources to accomplish agreed upon purposes. This increment of power, as compared with anything rulers of the Old Regime had been able to command, provided the ultimate argument that made the revolutionary changes irreversible, and indeed, forced even Napoleon's (ruled 1799–1815) most inveterate enemies to imitate at least some of the innovations the revolution had brought.

Speaking generally, what the French revolutionaries did was to sweep away obstacles to manipulation of men and resources by a single national command center. Peculiar local practices and immunities were systematically suppressed. Administrative uniformity brought equal taxation in all parts of the country; this meant a vast increment of disposable income at the center. After revolutionary legislation had been codified and applied throughout France, individual citizens confronted the august embodiment of the Nation, as it were, face to face, without the protecting integument of corporate identities and roles which had all (except the Church) been swept away as part of the abominable aristocratic privilege that had hamstrung French government for so long. In actual fact, what a citizen confronted was an agent of the central government—whether representative-on-mission, prefect, tax collector, or recruiting sergeant—who, in the name of the People, demanded goods and services on a far more massive scale than royal agents had ever been able to command. But as citizens, bone of one bone with the sovereign People from whom all authority descended, loyal Frenchmen had no logical recourse; and most of them did as they were told willingly enough.

The enhanced power such a regime could attain was most clearly apparent in military matters. The right to command the services of all adult males as soldiers was taken for granted by the hard pressed Convention in 1793 when it decreed the famous *Levée en masse*. Other societies had acted on the same assumption in the past—the Roman republic not least, which in fact offered the revolutionaries their favorite historical model. But the art of war as developed in Europe between 1650 and 1789 had made universal conscription inconceivable. A few had specialized as soldiers; most merely paid taxes to support them. The innovation of the revolutionary era was to make something close to universal military service for men of active years possible by expanding production of military supplies at home and by relying on captured material and the conscripted manufacturing resources of most of Europe to supply the swollen French forces. Where before the division of labor between soldier and civilian had been organized within national and state boundaries, under Napoleon the tendency was for French soldiers (and soldiers in French service from other nations) to rely on the rest of continental Europe for their support.

An enormous increase in the size of armies was one result. Short, decisive compaigns were another, for such enormous armies could not long remain in the field, being too large to survive on supplies brought up regularly from the rear. Nevertheless, a series of swift, sudden victories, followed by replenishment of supplies at the expense of the conquered army and population allowed vast French forces to remain in existence for something like twenty years, until Napoleon found himself lured onto ground where local resources were inadequate for the support of really large armies—that is, Spain to the south and Russia to the east.

Among Napoleon's enemies, too, an international division of labor asserted itself strongly. Austria, Prussia, and Russia, on-again, off-again allies of Great Britain against Napoleon, maintained larger armies than their own resources would have permitted thanks to British subsidies. These payments permitted the respective continental governments and/or peoples to buy British-made goods on an enhanced scale needed for prosecuting the war.

Thus the two leading nations of western Europe played fundamentally contrasting roles between 1792 and 1815. The French specialized as soldiers and administrators and drew support from a broad band of adjacent German and Italian territory; the British specialized in manufacturers for (among other customers) the rulers and soldiers of central and eastern Europe.

Of the two, the British role proved the more durable. French domination, however disguised by revolutionary phrases, inevitably galled the pride of those they subjugated. Moreover, revolutionary principles were double edged: if fraternity made Frenchmen so powerful, perhaps a touch of the same elixir would produce similar results for Spaniards or even for the much put-upon, constantly-fought-over Germans. German national sentiment was in fact very effectually stirred up against the French in 1813–14. Such appeals to nationalist feeling were not the least of the ways in which royalty learned from revolutionaries how to mobilize popular support more effectively than before.

The British, on the other hand, expanded their industrial capacity very rapidly throughout the wars, and when peace came they were in a position to supply more and cheaper goods than anyone else—an advantage which not all governments and states were prepared to pass up, though some did set up tariffs and quotas aimed at shutting out British manufactures. Despite these reactions to their dominating economic position, the British emerged as the "workshop of the world," whereas after 1815 France was no longer the ruler of Europe —merely a threat to its political stability, against which the monarchs and peoples of the rest of Europe stood keenly on guard.

Yet on a longer time scale, the innovations of ideal and practice in politics associated with the French Revolution and the innovations of industrial organization and practice associated with the English industrial revolution of the latter eighteenth century were alike inasmuch as both proved exportable; and once well rooted beyond their original heartland, their spread diluted the primacy they had initially conferred upon France and Britain.

There is another significant parallel between the French Revolution and the industrial revolution. For just as the ultimate success of revolutionary principles had been validated by the superior power they allowed the French government to exert, so, too, the industrial changes that took place in England and Scotland from 1750 to 1850 or thereabouts also multiplied the power available to Europeans in many different ways: technological, military, economic, and political. Indeed, the industrial revolution may be defined as the result of systematic application of inanimate power to manufacturing, transport, and communications. Since inanimate sources of power were potentially far greater than muscle power and could be applied on a vast scale once appropriate machines had been invented, older limits upon the quantity of goods men could produce were lifted. Many of Europe's more optimistic thinkers quickly fastened upon the new-found possibility of abundance (or at least material sufficiency) for all and pinned high hopes upon socialist transformation and/or revolution. By the end of the nineteenth century, for many industrial workers such hopes had displaced the older Christian hope of salvation.

Two aspects of the industrial revolution seem worth emphasizing here. First was the way in which Britain and the rest of industrializing Europe met the problem of finding sufficient food and fuel to support rapidly growing urban populations. Throughout the nineteenth century coal was the all-important fuel, and location of heavy industry was governed by the location of coal measures. These stretched in an irregular belt across Europe from Wales and Scotland, through Belgium and Westphalia to Silesia, the Don Basin and on into central Asia in Kazakstan. The diffusion of the industrial revolution from the British midlands, where it mainly originated, to Belgium, Germany, and Russia was in large measure due to the successive exploitation of more and more easterly coal fields. When other fuels became important—oil in the early twentieth century, uranium more recently—Europe lost the advantages of easy access to cheap fuel which had helped maintain its initial industrial primacy. Methods of mining and prospecting for coal and other minerals underwent considerable elaboration; and the uses to which coal was put also widened with the discovery of coking in the eighteenth century and of coal tar chemistry in the nineteenth. Coking was particularly important, for it allowed coal to be used as fuel for smelting iron and steel, thus freeing Europe from its earlier dependency on charcoal for that process.

Food was obviously just as critical to the progress of industrialization as fuel. On the one hand, improved transport and marketing arrangements attracted food to the growing industrial centers from ever greater distances. Prior to 1870, mobilization of agricultural surplus for the support of industrial populations was largely confined to the continent of Europe. Greater and greater quantities of grain came westward from the valleys of the Vistula, Danube, Dnieper, and Don rivers. After 1870, American and other overseas grain fields began to supply British and continental Europe (insofar as tariffs did not prevent it) with a flood of comparatively cheap grain. This pattern still persists.

The other way in which Europe met the food supply problem was by intensification of more local production of food stuffs. Numerous improvements in farming methods increased yields substantially, chief among them being use of chemical fertilizers (from the 1840's) and more carefully selected seed. But the spread of two American food crops—potatoes in northern Europe and maize in the hotter and dryer south—was the single most important step in increasing Europe's own food production. In the early stages of the industrial revolution, potatoes were particularly important, since in the climate of northwestern Europe (and especially in sandy soils ill-suited to grain) potatoes yielded up to four times as many calories per acre as had been attainable before. In particular, Germany's industrialization would have been impossible without the burgeoning potato fields that spread throughout the country from the time of the Seven Years' War, 1756–63. During that hard fought struggle thousands upon thousands of peasants discovered that potatoes could be left in the fields through the winter months and dug up as needed. Such a crop was almost safe from military requisitioning unless the soldiers had time to dig them hill by hill. Grain, on the other hand, had to be harvested and stored in a barn where the first foraging party to arrive could demand the delivery of an entire year's crop in the name of the king, offering, at best, a dubiously negotiable chit of paper in return.

These technical and marketing changes were important in themselves; but their combined impact upon traditional agricultural patterns of life in Europe and beyond that continent's limits added up to more than the sum of the parts. Prior to

1750, most cities had drawn subsistence from the countryside by a combination of rents and taxes. Supplies and services rendered by city folk to the peasant cultivators in return for deliveries of food were slight or nonexistent. With the progress of the industrial revolution, however, a growing variety of urban products came onto the market which were better and cheaper than anything peasant households could produce themselves or get from village artisans and local handicraft specialists. Cheap cotton cloth was the first and chiefest of such commodities; but in time innumerable other things followed from kerosene and kerosene lamps to tractors.

Availability of these commodities altered rural life profoundly. Village and small town artisan occupations disappeared, sometimes at great cost in human suffering. The autonomy and isolation of village life weakened rapidly. By degrees urban ideas and aspirations filtered into the peasant populations, producing, as often as not, violent discontent with traditional rural conditions. Particularly in eastern Europe, peasant discontents found incandescent political expression in nationalist and revolutionary movements beginning about 1870; but everywhere in Europe the older gap between town and country narrowed, village self-sufficiency diminished, and European agriculture, like European commerce and industry, began to respond to national and international market conditions, or, more recently, to the commands and blandishments of political managers and bureaucrats attempting to balance supply and demand for food (as for other commodities) by planning.

Of all the changes that have come to European and world society in the wake of the industrial revolution, this transformation of agricultural life seems likely to prove the most important. Ever since neolithic communities discovered how to extend natural grain fields by artificial means—digging and planting with seed—the majority of human beings have been subsistence farmers, with only marginal participation in economic or political structures that operated across large distances. The few exceptions to this rule—like the Athenian oil and wine producers of the fifth century B.C.—stand out against the anonymous mass of European and world peasantries whose lives involved only narrowly local relationships, and whose ethos and whole way of life depended on local traditions and face to face interactions within a village community. As the mass of European populations cut loose from such anchors, from the time of the English clearances and enclosures of the sixteenth and eighteenth centuries to the collectivization of post-World War II eastern Europe, a quite new balance of society set in. How stable or enduring it will be only the future will show. But by breaking down peasant patterns of life across the whole of Europe within a mere two centuries, the industrial revolution clearly severed the mass of European mankind from age-old ancestral ways of life. It may well require another two centuries or longer before any comparably stable adjustment to the altered realities of human interdependence emerges—if it ever does.

A second aspect of the industrial revolution that seems worthwhile underlining here is the importance of war and mobilization for war in provoking departures from familiar manufacturing routines and especially in expanding scale of production. In the eighteenth century, military demand acted like a vast bellows speeding up reactions of every kind in the industrial sector of the British economy. The Seven Years' War was a landmark: it required a more strenuous mobilization of home resources than Britain had ever before undertaken; and the pattern of subsidy to the Prussians, allowing Frederick the Great to maintain a larger army than he could otherwise have done, set a precedent for the longer and more important subsidies of the Napoleonic period.

Cutbacks and abrupt discontinuance of government orders

were almost as important as sudden increases in demand from the same source. Such cutbacks tended to weed out the inefficient firms, while technologically progressive and well-managed organizations were compelled to find civilian markets for their products, at least until a new round of government orders restored sudden prosperity for all and invited technological shortcuts to meet a suddenly enlarged demand. Civilian enterprise and marketing of course mattered; indeed, in some lines, like cotton manufacture, which was one of the most dramatic aspects of the British industrial revolution, the civilian sector clearly predominated. Only by giving due weight to other manufactures, some of which increased in scale without altering technology very notably, does the role of government orders and military markets become apparent. Moreover, subsidy payments to foreign governments opened markets in Europe for cotton cloth, as well as for other commodities which were not purchased directly by military or official agents, but circulated instead through civilian channels of trade.

The worldwide as well as pan-European importance of the industrial revolution scarely needs to be emphasized. Generally speaking, it is approximately true that before 1750 the margin Europeans had over other civilized peoples of the world was primarily naval and military. When it came to trade, the artisan products of Moslem, Indian, and Chinese workshops commanded a larger market in Europe than European manufactures could command in Asia. Woolen cloth (in cooler regions) plus raw metals (of which Europeans had a superior supply thanks to their expertness as miners) were about all that civilized foreigners found worth buying from the west. As a result, force and threat of force constituted an important element in European overseas trade throughout the Old Regime. In particular, compulsory labor played a very conspicuous part in European overseas economic activity both in the form of the slave plantations of the New World and in the form of semifree artisan and agricultural production in India and Indonesia.

After about 1750, however, and definitively by 1800, European (read British) workshops were in a position to offer cheaper and better goods than local artisans could produce, even in such civilized regions as India and the Middle East. By about 1850 or so the same was true of China. This allowed European penetration of the Asian and African continents to proceed more rapidly and in a different fashion than before. Cheap European goods upset social structures wherever artisan populations had been important. Distressed artisans who could not compete in price and/or quality with imported European goods provoked acute internal conflicts; such disorders facilitated and sometimes invited European political-military intervention.

In other words, the processes through which European peasants and artisans were induced and compelled to abandon accustomed patterns of behavior manifested themselves with scarcely diminished and only slightly delayed force overseas and across civilizational boundaries. The effect was to weaken, indeed almost to paralyze, traditional political leadership in most parts of the globe, enormously facilitating the nineteenth century growth of European overseas empires. Just as local, village autonomies diminished to the vanishing point under the assault of machine-made goods and all that went with them, so also the autonomy of Asian and African cultures and civilizations crumbled before the same forces. Worldwide as well as pan-European interaction and interdependence assumed hitherto unimagined intensity as a result.

Within Europe between 1815 and 1870, the political and legal upheavals connected with the French Revolution and the economic upheavals connected with the industrial revolution tended to go together. Individuals and groups actively promoting one sort of change often supported the other too; opponents, similarly, tended to resist both. Yet there was no necessary connection between liberal and democratic forms of government and industrialism. This gradually became apparent in the course of the nineteenth century. In the Balkans and in Russia, for instance, industrialism implanted by government fiat and financed by foreign capital outran liberal patterns of government; simultaneously liberal political ideals and practice outdistanced industrialism in Italy and uncertainly also in Spain.

Yet to most observers in the nineteenth century itself, manifestations of the fragility of the connection between political liberalism and industrialism seemed unimportant, atypical, and could be attributed to transitory deficiencies in local skills and traditions. Most western Europeans agreed, after the convulsion of the Napoleonic period had subsided, that even if constitutions and political command structures were man-made and thus subject to human will, there still remained a "natural" economic order which functioned best when human nature and calculated individual self-interest directed behavior. According to this "liberal" vision of the human condition, governments ought to leave economic processes alone insofar as possible; private persons, pursuing what they saw to be their own best interest, could be trusted to manage the economy better than it could be managed by any government official.

Complete laissez faire never existed, even in Great Britain where the doctrine was strongest and where traditions of administrative control of behavior were weaker than anywhere else in Europe. Moreover, as more and more people began to live in towns and work in industry or related service occupations, a host of new corporate bodies began to grow, within which individuals eagerly sought refuge from the uncertainties and hardships of industrial urbanization. This was especially true in the parts of western Europe where industrialization was oldest. Larger and larger business enterprises, legally incorporated so as to assume many of the legal rights of a person, were only one of the new forms of corporate life—though a very important one. There were in addition a veritable forest of benevolent and self-help societies, municipal government agencies, labor unions, social gatherings like the chapels and pubs of Great Britain, together with socialist and other political parties (especially on the continent) that grew up within the context of the new industrial cities and towns.

These and other corporate bodies began to cushion the naked confrontation of the national state with its individual citizens which had been so pronounced in the first stages of the French Revolution. By 1914 in western and central Europe the new complex of privileged corporations and vested interests had become quite as formidable as those of the Old Regime. The new organizations often had the effect of slowing down the pace of industrial change and tended to reduce the personal strain and the socio-economic disasters that industrialism, especially in its early phases, had sometimes provoked.

After about 1870, a slow down of British economic development set in, at least by comparison with what happened in the newer industrial centers of Germany and the United States. The Americans recapitulated the British model of industrialization and improved upon it mainly by enlarging the scale of operation. Larger markets, larger machinery, larger business organizations, greater raw material resources, a more elastic labor force thanks to mass immigration from Europe: in these and similar respects the United States far outstripped the British between 1870 and 1914.

Quantitatively, the Germans also surpassed the British in many lines of production by 1914. More important for the future, though, was the fact that the Germans departed from British patterns of industrialization in some important ways. First of all, the roles of government officials and of a handful of great banks that worked hand in hand with government was far greater in Germany than had been the case in Great Britain. The role of officialdom was even greater in Russia, when that country began to industrialize on a significant scale after 1890; the same was true of Japan. Indeed, in the twentieth century it became clear that the German pattern of active manipulation of economic policy by an educated elite of government officials and managerial experts was a far more viable export model for industrialism than was the original British pattern, which left too much to private pecuniary initiatives of a kind that were either marginal or quite lacking in most societies.

A second way in which German industrial patterns differed from the British was the greater importance Germans accorded to advanced academic training in science and technology. Chemists, trained in university laboratories, began by inventing new coal tar dyes for each season's high fashion, so that a lady could appear annually in clothes of a hue literally never seen before. Ere long chemists discovered and learned how to mass produce other new substances as diverse and important as nitrogeneous fertilizers, dynamite, celluloid, and aspirin. Thanks largely to their superior educational system, Germans took and held the lead in such innovations. For the same reason, by 1914 the German artillery was bigger and better than anyone else's.

Yet even in Germany before World War I, the linkage between academic science and research on the one hand and industrial practice on the other was relatively weak. Prejudices on both sides prevented more than sporadic interaction between academic theorists and the grime and sweat of industrial processing. Many inventions resulted from the tinkering of some ingenious mechanic working by himself with meager capital and only an elementary education. Yet toward the very end of the nineteenth century a few big businesses began to set up laboratories where highly trained men were employed to improve existing techniques by testing alternatives systematically. Such research laboratories also kept looking, but only in rather unsystematic ways, for promising new applications of physical and chemical theory to manufacturing processes.

Britain's loss of industrial primacy about 1870 to Germany and the United States was matched by a similar eclipse of France and the political ideals associated with the French revolutionary and republican tradition. Defeat in the Franco-Prussian war (1870–71) led to the unification of Germany, not by the People under liberal leaders, but by Prince Otto von Bismarck (1815–98) and the Prussian army, acting in defiance of the expressed will of the elected representatives of the People. Simultaneously, the revolutionary rising of the People in Paris led to a violent parting of the ways between bourgeois republicans and socialist revolutionaries in France. Liberals and socialists in most of the rest of Europe soon followed suit. Thus the liberal, revolutionary, and republican ideals that had been handed down from 1793 split into jarring fragments, exactly at the time when an unrepentant reactionary, Chancellor Bismarck, showed how it was possible to manipulate public opinion so as to strengthen the power of kings and emperors, and other holdovers from Europe's Old Regime, by the very devices and instruments which had been the liberals' most reliable source of strength.

During the next half-century, European international politics turned on an effort to counterbalance the rising power of Germany by an alliance between political contraries: liberal France and Britain on the one hand and the Russian autocracy on the other. By 1907, when Britain, France, and Russia concluded a Triple Entente aimed at the containment of Germany, the polarity between liberal and reactionary, which had emerged from the French Revolution to define Europe's international alignments after 1815, had become outmoded.

In similar fashion, the liberal compromise between managed politics and "natural" economics, which had emerged after the Napoleonic wars, blurred and almost broke down. Economics was politicized in the name of social reform. Questions of economic policy tended to supplant constitutional quarrels as the most acrimonious foci of political debate.

The further east in Europe, the more active state officials became in all aspects of economic management. Russian industrialization and railroad building, for example, were state managed from the start. Revolutionary socialism and revolutionary nationalism also tended to become more persuasive as one went from west to east, since the managerial elites of eastern Europe were more authoritarian and systematically excluded certain national groups. By the end of the nineteenth century, Russia therefore presented the spectacle of two rival elites competing —often violently by bomb and hangman's noose—for control of the country's political and economic management. Ironically, the more successful the existing government was in advancing industrialization, the larger became the volatile urban population to whom socialist revolutionaries were able to appeal. In Ottoman and Hapsburg lands, on the other hand, revolutionary rhetoric found nationalist slogans more congenial, though the resultant political mobilization of lower against upper classes within existing social hierarchies was very similar to that which socialists so vigorously undertook in Germany and Russia.

Nevertheless, it took the human catastrophe of World War I to erase the boundary between politics and economics in all of Europe (except, perhaps, Switzerland) and to push the polarities of eastern Europe over the edge of revolution. By the end of the war, the United States had become the patron of nationalist revolution in southeast Europe, dragging the reluctant British and French governments along, whereas Russia had become the patron of class war, reproaching the desperately embarrassed socialist parties of western and central Europe for failure to join wholeheartedly in the revolutionary cause their spokesmen had so loudly and proudly proclaimed before 1914.

It is rash and perhaps unnecessary to say anything about the intellectual and cultural flowering of Europe in the nineteenth century. Institutional structures which deliberately encouraged innovative thoughts multiplied enormously. The outpouring of new ideas and projects was correspondingly vast. Professionalization ran rampant, so that the experts of one profession often lost touch with those of others. The result was pullulating confusion rather than any overarching intellectual structure, although just as there was a "European" art style until the first decade of the twentieth century that bound all the painters of Europe together in a loose but real way, so too there may have been a "European" intellectual style of which we are still too much a part to be able to recognize clearly.

Modern Europe's distinctive art style, inherited from Renaissance Italy, was discarded by avant garde painters in the decade before World War I when they rejected the master device of perspective and abandoned the ideal of making a painting resemble optical experience closely. In similar fashion, it is conceivable that future ages will recognize the abandonment of a long established "European" intellectual style at about the same time. Certainly, the discovery of unconscious levels of psychic activity and the still incomplete public recognition of the limitations on conscious management of human affairs created by irrational, subconscious levels of conduct marks a notable change in outlook. Yet reason has its way of outwitting unreason: the discovery of irrational levels of psychic life was itself a triumph of reasoning; and effective manipulation of such impulses to achieve consciously established goals is perhaps a reasonable dream, though the moral and practical dilemmas that actual achievement of such skills would create among men boggles the imagination. Who would manipulate whom? And for what purpose?

However future ages may assess the intellectual and artistic output of nineteenth century Europe, it seems sure that the massive variety of what was achieved will remain impressive. In retrospect it will probably appear as a European golden age when that small segment of the habitable globe dominated the entire world as no one center has ever done before, not merely politically and militarily, but far more significantly in scientific, technological, and intellectual matters.

The difficulty of passing anything like a firm and confident judgment upon nineteenth century European high culture is compounded as one comes closer to our own time. Political and social as well as intellectual and artistic events of the twentieth century are still too recent to allow any sort of confident analysis on a scale appropriate to a hasty overview of the whole of Europe's past such as this. Yet an attempt seems needful for completeness, even though the reader should understand how tentative any statements must be because the course of future events, which will surely give altered meaning to our recent past in times to come, remains unknowable.

As of 1973, at least, it looks as though Europe's political history since 1917 had been dominated by two conflicting yet complementary processes. One was the growth of American and Russian wealth, power, and influence. This tended to supplant the dominance northwestern Europe had exercised over all neighboring lands since 1600. On the other hand, the consolidation of western Europe into a trans-national political-economic unit tended to redress the balance in favor of the older metropolitan center. It is still too soon to know which way Europe's future will lastingly incline.

The United States and Russia began to catch up with western Europe industrially and in other respects before 1914.

This re-enacted a familiar frontier phenomenon. Peoples near the margins of a civilization have often been able to take advantage of access to larger blocs of territory. Applying techniques of manpower and resource management worked out at the metropolitan center to new ground and on a larger scale has repeatedly allowed such frontier polities to eclipse the power and wealth attainable by any one political unit at the center itself. In Europe's own history, for instance, this is what first Macedon and then Rome did to the Greek city-states of antiquity; and, as we have just seen, in the sixteenth century a similar fate overtook the the city-states of Italy at the hands of France, Spain, and Turkey.

The twentieth century variation upon this well worn theme of world history was remarkable mainly because of the way Russia has twice seemed about to catch up with western European nations only to fall behind again. As remarked above toward the end of the eighteenth century, Russia was clearly overtaking the organizational and technical levels of central and western Europe's Old Regime, only to be left behind by the new energies and resources so successfully tapped by the French Revolution on the one hand and by the industrial revolution on the other. In 1917, Russia had her own revolution, analogous to the French in the sense that the revolutionary regime soon proved able to mobilize for greater resources from the Russian population than the Tsars ever did. Moreover, the Communists have been eager to advance the industrial development of Russia, both for dogmatic reasons, and because industrial skills enormously enhance military and other forms of governmental power.

They have been marvelously successful, yet it is not clear that existing Russian command patterns will be able to bear the strain of conscripting human and material resources for state purposes indefinitely. Indeed, it is hard to see how the Communist Party can expect to pass on to future generations the ideals and aspirations that made the sacrifices of the revolutionary generation bearable, any more than the officials and landowners of Catherine II's time were able to pass on to their sons the attitudes that inspired the builders of Russia in the century after Peter the Great's revolutionary assault upon tradition.

Western Europe's twentieth century political development seems at least as remarkable as the rise of Russian and American powers centers. World War I quickly overturned the nineteenth century patterns of socio-economic management. Military conscription soon led the principal belligerent nations to planned allocations of civilian manpower too. Supply shortages at the front led to planned armaments production, raw material controls, fuel allocations, and so on. A command economy, in short, supplanted free market economic relations and acheived otherwise impossible results. In principle, though reality of course always fell short, it was as though an entire nation coalesced into a single vast business enterprise, managed to maximize output of war goods and services.

The brutal result, involving the squalid death of millions in the trenches of the western front, led French and British governments between the wars to reject the new managerial roles they had explored during the war. In Russia, however, from the time the first Five Year Plan was instituted (1928), the Communist regime made the sort of economic command planning that had been used in western nations during World War I a normal peace-time condition. Soon thereafter, Nazi and New Deal responses to the Depression of the 1930's introduced less drastic but nonetheless real variations of the wartime economic model into Germany and the United States.

World War II (1939–45) widened the range of mobilization and improved upon World War I methods in two main respects. First of all, transnational coordination became normal. The British and Americans managed a common war effort particularly well between 1941 and 1945, and by 1944, the the Russians, too, depended in important ways on supplies delivered from the United States. The American government thus re-enacted the role the British government had played in Europe during the Napoleonic wars, subsidizing the Russians (and other "United Nations") so that they could maintain larger armed forces in the field than would have been possible on the strength of local resources alone. The resulting increase in overall allied military efficiency was substantial, but this did nothing to assure maintenance of the alliance system once the common enemy had been defeated. The breakup of the alliance against Napoleon after 1818 was therefore re-enacted after 1947 when the Grand Alliance of World War II turned into the aptly named Cold War.

It was not only among Hitler's enemies that transnational management won striking successes during World War II. Nazi racial and nationalist doctrines notwithstanding, the European continent also witnessed a remarkable transnational economic and administrative integration during the latter phases of World War II. Having conquered most of Europe by 1942, the Nazis began to draw upon the manpower and material resources of the entire area under their command to supply German armies. Their position therefore resembled that of the French during the Napoleonic wars, with this difference that Hitler's professed political principles were repulsive to all who could not qualify as members of the master race, so that the appeal which French revolutionary ideals had exerted upon fraternal (if subject) peoples was almost totally lacking within Nazi-dominated Europe.

Yet memories of Europe's war-time economic pattern could not be wiped away. When economic boom conditions returned to western Europe after 1948, men who had worked as slave laborers in German factories during the war were ready enough to return to Germany again as factory workers. Thousands of others followed. More generally, the postwar success of the Common Market was surely facilitated by recollections of the massive transnational migrations that had taken place during the war, when soldiers and prisoners of war as well as civilian slave laborers had criss-crossed Europe's national boundaries by the hundreds of thousands. The breakdown of Europe's national barriers thus appears as the ironic and altogether unexpected but probably most lasting monument to Hitler's (ruled 1933–45) career.

The second way in which World War II mobilization improved upon earlier patterns was the greater scope planners gave to systematic, organized invention. To be sure, there were beginnings in 1916–18, when rapid evolution of airplane design and the creation of such a radically new weapon as the tank took place. But deliberate invention remained marginal in World War I. In 1939–45, on the contrary, all major belligerents invested much effort in planning new weapons. They achieved some startling results. The most dramatic and important was the controlled release of nuclear energy (1942–45). Other major inventions—rockets, jet airplanes, radar, and the like—came into being under similar circumstances, as a result of systematic collaboration between academic theorists and the best engineers and technologists that could be assembled and set to work on the task.

The effect of such organized invention was to reverse older relationships between inventor and the marketing of his invention. Under the pressure of war needs, men first decided what was needed to accomplish some purpose, then assigned experts to solve the technical problems inherent in producing a suitable device that would have the desired performance characteristics. The ultimate consumers waited impatiently until the tangible product of such inventive collaboration finally became available. Instead of an isolated "crackpot" inventor having to overcome systematic resistance to his proposed innovation, now change was taken for granted, actively desired by the managerial elite, and facilitated by everything administrative action could achieve.

Planned economies and planned invention proved relatively easy to achieve in war. The goal of victory and the steps likely to contribute to it were relatively clear to all concerned, as well as being acceptable to almost everyone—on both sides. In peace, agreement was far harder to achieve. Hence, planned mobilization of manpower and resources remained sporadic in western Europe and was mainly confined to the design and redesign of weapons systems. But business corporations, military planners, and social reformers all recognized what could be done by large-scale concentration of effort and intelligence for devising new ways of doing things. The malleability of society and of economic relations seemed about as great as the malleability of governmental forms. This made choices difficult, while depriving custom of claim to more than tentative legitimacy.

Despite all such uncertainties, since 1948 the heartland of western European civilization has prospered greatly. In intellectual and technical matters Europe is not noticeably laggard in comparison with anywhere else, except, perhaps, Japan. The loss of political control over colonies in Africa and Asia did little to diminish European wealth and power. On the contrary, the ex-imperial governments were spared heavy expenditures which would have been necessary to maintain increasingly unpopular regimes. In eastern Europe, to be sure, Russian armies and political agents set up a kind of semi-colonial regime immediately after World War II, supplementing a fully colonial regime the Russian government maintained in central Asia. This (with the Chinese the sole surviving political empire of the globe) still stands.

The activity of United States diplomats, soldiers, and businessmen in western Europe (and elsewhere in the world) also created an informal sort of empire after World War II, though American influence, at least in Europe, was on the whole less heavy handed than that of the Russians in the eastern satellite lands. As of 1973, however, it is not clear that Europeans, both those located in the Russian sphere of influence and those living in the American ambit, will not again assert their effective independence. The nationalism of eastern European peoples seems able to inhibit effective transnational economic integration among the Communist states—despite Marxist internationalist principles. In contrast, the growing solidity of transnational structures in western Europe—if the process of consolidation continues for another generation or longer—may create a power center comprising the French, British, German, and Italian nations, together with a fringe of others, whose strength would compare favorably with that of any in the world. Hence, whatever the future may prove, it now seems premature to suppose that the old centers of European civilization have exhausted their creative power.

For this reason, and because with the spread of industrialism and of modern patterns of economic and political management, all the earth has in some measure become the heir of European thought and technology, study of, and reflection upon, the shape of European history seems still worthwhile.

INDEX

EUROPE
0
400
Miles
ATLANTIC OCEAN
BRITISH ISLES
NORTH SEA
Dublin
Humber R.
London
Thames R.
Amsterdam
Antwerp
ENGLISH CHANNEL
Oslo
Stockholm
Copenhagen
BALTIC SEA
Danzig
Hamburg
Weser R.
Berlin
Warsaw
Oder R.
Elbe R.
Rhine R.
Frankfurt am Main
Prague
Vistula R.
Seine R.
Paris
Loire R.
BAY OF BISCAY
Danube R.
Vienna
Zurich
ALPS
Budapest
Milan
Venice
Drava R.
Sava R.
Theiss R.
Garonne R.
Rhone R.
PYRENEES
Genoa
Po R.
Florence
Douro R.
Ebro R.
Lisbon
Tagus R.
Madrid
ADRIATIC SEA
Tiber R.
APENNINES
CORSICA
Rome
BALEARIC ISLANDS
SARDINIA
Guadalquivir R.
PINDUS
MEDITERRANE
SICILY
Algiers
Rabat
Tunis
ATLAS MOUNTAINS